HELEN HIEBERT

PLAYING WITH POP-UPS

THE ART OF DIMENSIONAL, MOVING PAPER DESIGNS

Quarry Books
100 Cummings Center, Suite 406L
Beverly, MA 01915

quarrybooks.com • craftside.typepad.com

First published in the United States of America by
Quarry Books, a member of
Quayside Publishing Group
100 Cummings Center
Suite 406-L
Beverly, Massachusetts 01915-6101
Telephone: (978) 282-9590
Fax: (978) 283-2742
www.quarrybooks.com
Visit www.Craftside.Typepad.com for a behind-the-scenes peek at our crafty world!

Library of Congress Cataloging-in-Publication Data available

ISBN: 978-1-59253-908-6

Digital edition published in 2014
eISBN: 978-1-62788-032-9

10 9 8 7 6 5 4 3 2 1

Cover images (top to bottom; left to right): *Hide and Seek*, David Carter; *Bloodroot Plant*, Shawn Sheehy; *Untitled*, Peter Dahmen; *Pop-Up Tent and Pyramid*, Carol Barton
Cover & Book Design: Landers Miller Design
Photography: Zach Mahone Photography, step shots; Glenn Scott Photography, project photos
Templates: © Individual artists
Templates on pages 25; 29; 33; 120 (top); 121–122 illustrated by Mattie S. Wells
Photos, page 4, (top to bottom; left to right): *Tender Pixel*, Elod Beregszaszi; *The 12 Days of Christmas*, Robert Sabuda; *Untitled*, Hand Papermaking, Inc.; *Peacock*, Peter Dahmen
Access downloadable project templates at: www.quarrybooks.com/pages/pop-ups

Printed in China

TITLE: POP-UP CONCERTINA
ARTIST: Shelby Arnold
DESCRIPTION: Printed card stock, accordion folded with hand-cut pop-ups. 6" x 38" (15.2 x 96.5 cm) wide when opened up flat, 6" x 3¾" x ½" (15.2 x 9.5 x 1.3 cm) folded, the Pop-Up Concertina was printed in an edition of 1,000. Each copy is hand-cut and folded by the artist. The Pop-Up Concertina is an accordion-folded booklet with cut-out pop-ups, covered on both sides with detailed pen illustrations. As the viewer manipulates the pages into different configurations, the cut-outs, folds, and illustrations interact in various combinations.

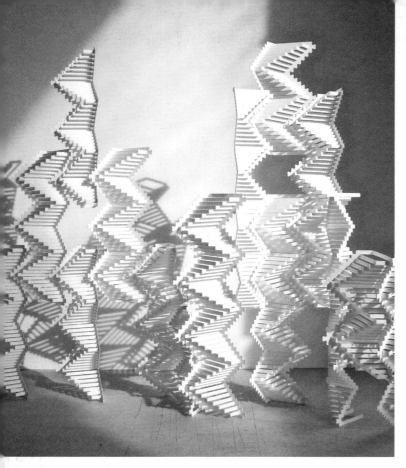

CONTENTS

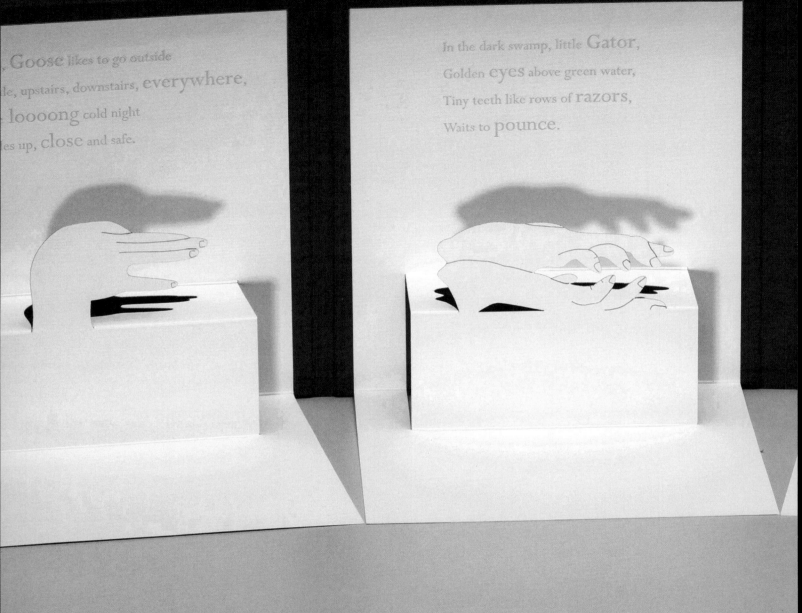

Goose likes to go outside
de, upstairs, downstairs, everywhere,
loooong cold night
es up, close and safe.

In the dark swamp, little Gator,
Golden eyes above green water,
Tiny teeth like rows of razors,
Waits to pounce.

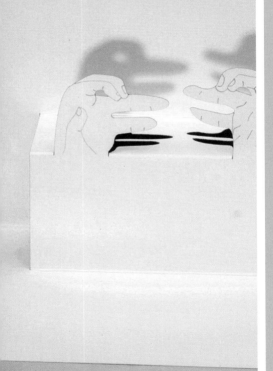

Baby birds in a tree-top nest d...

That when they grow, they will b...

Now they argue and wait for Dad...

To bring a nice chewy minnow to s...

Introduction

During my junior year abroad in Germany, I took a class in letter-forms and became enamored with a font called Block Up.

I found a two-dimensional rendering of this three-dimensional alphabet so intriguing that I set out to fabricate the block letters in three dimensions—literally. Soon afterward, I discovered origamic architecture (OA), a Japanese form of paper sculpture. I returned from Germany and created a series of sculptures based on OA techniques I learned by studying the few books on the subject and created my first body of work for my college art thesis based on the art form.

After college, I moved to New York City and my love of working with paper continued. During a brief trip to Japan, I fell in love with hand papermaking and dedicated myself to learning all about that craft, which I was able to do by landing a job at Dieu Donné Papermill in New York City. And along the way, I discovered book arts and took courses from masters in the field at the New York Center for Book Arts. Fast-forward almost twenty years, and just last year, I produced my first limited edition pop-up book, *The Pop-Up Hand Shadow Book*. The pop-ups come to life when the viewer shines a flashlight on the pop-up animals, casting shadows onto the pages.

When given the opportunity to write this book, I decided the best approach would be to ask paper engineers from around the world to contribute projects. Thankfully, they were up to the task and designed a smashing array of projects that will introduce you to a wide variety of pop-up techniques. The gallery section at the back of the book shows off the professional work of these amazing artists and serves to inspire. When talking with the top paper engineers in the field, I was pleased to discover that most of them begin each new project armed with paper, scissors, and glue or tape—that's it! Knowing that, my deduction is that we are all capable of paper engineering if we put our minds to it, and I have no doubt that there are countless pop-ups waiting to be born!

TITLE: THE POP-UP HAND SHADOW BOOK
DESCRIPTION: The Pop-Up Hand Shadow Book features four illustrated animal hand shadows in a theatrical book structure. The animals are brought to life as the viewer plays with a mini flashlight (packaged with the book), casting shadows onto panels behind the pop-ups. A verse about each animal, by poet Nora Robertson, appears on each page; letterpress printed and laser cut paper pages, book board, book cloth, cherry & plywood laser cut box;
Box: 6¾" x 7⅜" x 1¼" (17 x 19 x 3 cm); Book: 6¹⁄₁₆" x 6⅛" x ¾" (15.2 x 15.4 x 2 cm);
Extended: 6¹⁄₁₆" x 18" x 8" (15.2 x 45.7 x 20.3 cm).
PHOTO: DAN KVITKA

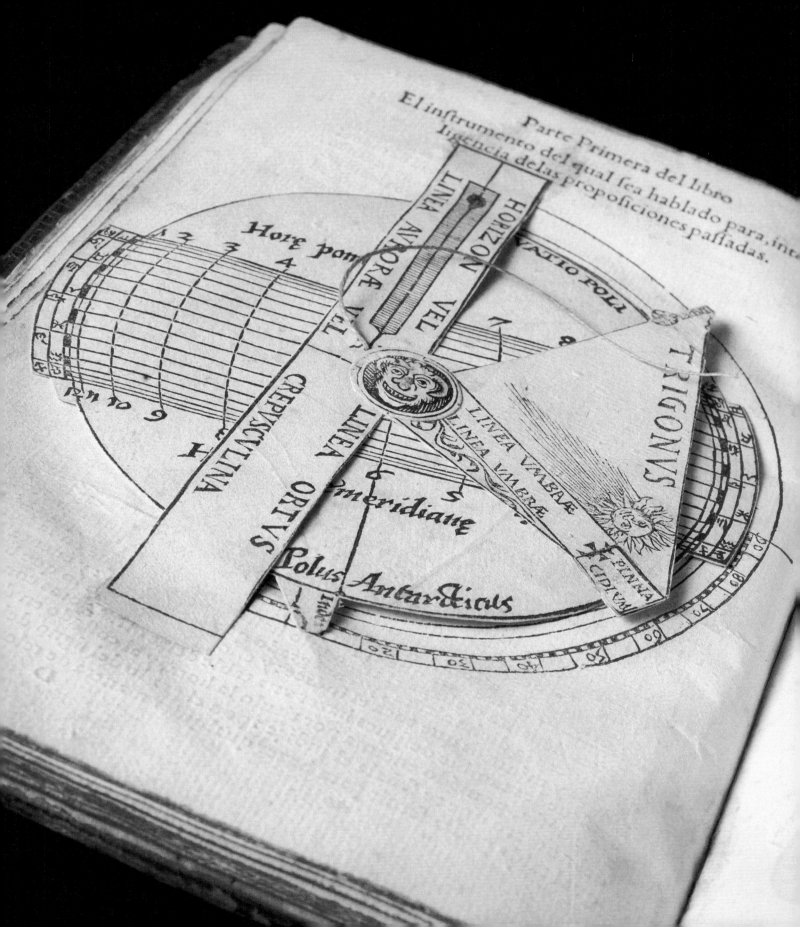

CHAPTER 1

Getting Started: Cut, Score, Fold, Pop!

Pop-ups are magical. As children's book author Robert Sabuda says, there is a "wow" factor involved when you open a page and something moves. It is surprising . . . exciting . . . it's magic! Adults and children alike are enchanted as they watch a scene literally unfold—a dragon popping out of a page, a tower rising up from the paper's surface, or a word springing from between the folds.

Created in 1548, *Libro dela Cosmographia* by Peter Apian is an incredible example of one of the earliest volvelles created. Owned by the University of Rochester's Rush Rhees Library, Department of Rare Books and Special Collections.

PHOTO: J. ADAM FENSTER/UNIVERSITY OF ROCHESTER

A Brief History of Pop-Ups

Pop-ups and movables have a surprisingly long history. Some of the earliest movables were created in the thirteenth century in the form of volvelles, rotating paper disks, which were simple calendars (try your hand at making a volvelle, see page 85). Flaps that were adhered to a page and could be lifted to reveal something underneath were another early invention, commonly used in anatomical illustrations. Soon, a variety of mechanisms started appearing on the pages of books, bringing them to life, such as hinged flaps that folded out of the page and shaped pieces that pulled out of pockets. Tunnel books (you can make your own, see page 76) appeared in the eighteenth century, evolving from traveling peep shows that were often carried on the backs of showmen.

Up until this time, movable books were almost always educational and geared toward adults. In the nineteenth century, children's pop-up books came into vogue, and companies in England and other parts of Europe set up specialized departments for hand assembly. Some notable names from the early days are Ernest Nister, a nineteenth-century German publisher who, among other things, produced movables with dissolving images, in which a pull tab enables one set of images to slide over another.

The first company in the United States to produce movable books was McLoughlin Brothers of New York. Blue Ribbon, an American publishing house founded in 1930, actually registered the term *pop-up* to describe movable illustrations, and paper engineering branched out to include greeting cards and advertising around this time as well.

Czechoslovakian artist Vojtech Kubasta was an innovator in the field around the middle of the century, developing new mechanisms and illustrating shaped books with windows cut out of the covers, as well as large-format pop-ups.

During the 1960s, book packagers (companies that coordinate entire book projects, from conception to shipping) helped revive the pop-up book industry, which had slowed down during World War II and the Great Depression. The term *paper engineer* became official, and paper engineers began receiving credit for their work. In the 1980s, numerous pop-up books wielding innovative engineering were produced, and the term *pop-up* became a household term.

Title: *UNTITLED (Father Christmas) by Vojtech Kubasta,* MID-1950s
Description: Large 13" × 9" (33 × 22 cm) double-page pop-up showing Santa with a bag of toys approaching a house. Tabs on the cover slide from side to side moving the eyes and mouth of Father Christmas.
PHOTO: ANN MONTANARO

Pop-Ups Today

Currently, there are pop-up books for children and adults ranging in theme from the simple to the sublime, and paper engineers continue to develop amazing creations to knock our socks off. There are pop-up greeting cards that incorporate sound and light (see Jie Qi's work on page 114) and innovations in advertising that incorporate Wi-Fi into print communication.

One other form of pop-up that began in the 1980s and deserves recognition is origamic architecture; its development is attributed to professor Masahiro Chatani (1934–2008) of Japan. Chatani's experiments with cutting and folding, accompanied by his experience in architectural design, led to a distinct form of pop-ups, engaging shadow play, utilizing repetitive forms, and featuring elegant paper sculptures cut in plain white card stock. Chatani published more than fifty books on origamic architecture, exhibited his work, and frequently collaborated with Keiko Nakazawa and Takaaki Kihara, who are both still active in the field today. There are also protégés around the world who practice the technique of origamic architecture (see the work of Elod Beregszaszi on page 100).

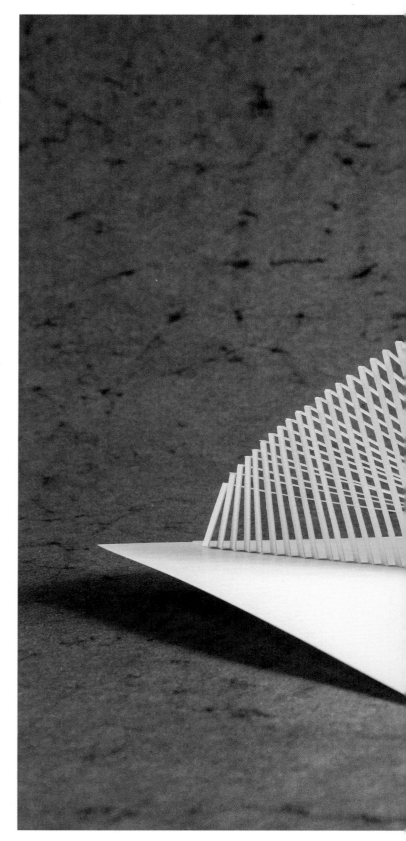

Title: *INFINITY*
Description: Pop-up greeting card designed by Masahiro Chatani. Countless lines produce 3-D space beyond reality, 4" × 8½" × 6½" (10.2 × 21.6 × 16.5 cm).

Terminology: What Is a Pop-Up/How Are Pop-Up Mechanisms Defined?

In general, pop-ups appear between a fold or crease in a piece of paper and are activated as the viewer unfolds a page. There are many different mechanisms that can make this happen, and there is no formal dictionary of pop-up terms. Some people call the same mechanism by different names (for example, a **twister** can be called a **transformer** or **opposing angles with a tent**). A good visual guide to terminology (featuring actual pop-ups) can be found in David Carter and Jim Diaz's book *The Elements of Pop-Up*.

Movable books and **paper engineering** are broader terms that include other types of mechanisms that do not interact with the turn of a page, such as a pull tab or a **volvelle** (a rotating disk). A few of the projects in this book (the Puppy, the Volvelle, and the Rib Cage) are not true pop-ups, but incorporate paper engineering techniques and are considered movables.

A **paper engineer** is someone who designs pop-up or movable books, pop-up greeting cards, or pop-ups for advertising. Pop-ups have even been engineered for record and CD cases and have appeared on film sets.

The Anatomy of a Pop-Up

Here is a list of the parts of a pop-up, as well as common tasks you will perform to create your own.

Folio, spread, or **base card:** the folded page spread on which a pop-up is built **(A)**.

Mountain fold: when paper is folded so that it looks like a mountain peak when resting on a surface **(B)**.

Valley fold: when paper is folded so that it looks like a valley or the letter *V* when resting on a surface **(C)**.

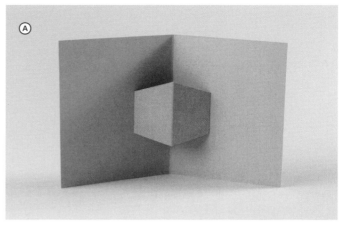

Folio, spread, or base card

Mountain fold

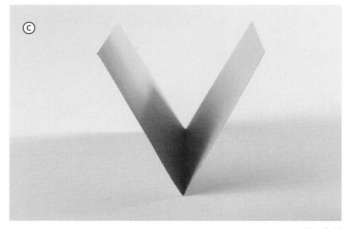

Valley fold

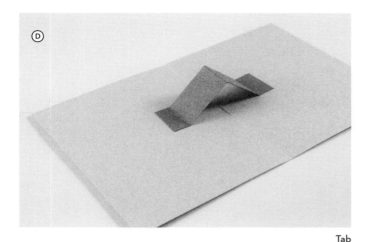

Tab

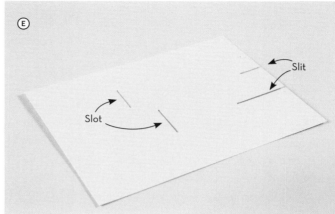

Slit and Slot

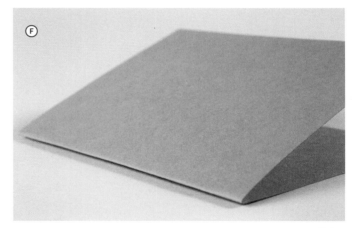

Spine

Score line

Template: The patterns in the back of the book are templates. They can be enlarged and cut out to create the pop-up projects in this book. The templates also can be found online at www.quarrybooks.com/pages/pop-ups.

Mechanism: a movable or pop-up structure.

Tab: a small flap of paper that is glued to connect one part of a pop-up to the base card or to another piece of paper **(D)**.

Slit: a cut, usually perpendicular to the edge of a sheet of paper **(E)**.

Slot: a thin line cut within a sheet, into which another sheet of paper or a tab can be slipped **(E)**.

Spine: When a sheet of card stock is folded in half, the folded edge is often referred to as the spine **(F)**.

Score line: a dent in card stock made with a scoring tool that helps the paper fold sharply and accurately. You can score a sheet of paper by running a bone folder (or another blunt object such as a paper clip) along a straightedge and pressing into the paper as you do so, creasing the paper and enabling it to fold easily along the scored line **(G)**.

THE PRODUCTION OF A POP-UP

Quite a bit of innovation went on during the last part of the twentieth century as paper engineers and book packagers figured out how to fabricate dies for cutting pop-ups and set up assembly lines for hand assembly. Basic paper engineering is still done by hand with paper, tape, and scissors. Some parts of the process have been computerized (illustration and layout, for example) but the actual assembly of pop-ups is still done by hand. Following are the steps from conception to completion.

An idea is developed and a storyboard is submitted to a publisher (A).

A prototype is produced as the paper engineer creates two- and three-dimensional sketches and performs the paper engineering (B).

Illustrations and type are added (C).

Once the publisher approves the idea, the paper engineering is refined to make it as simple as possible (with production and cost in mind) while still getting the message across (D).

A sample is cut on a plotter cutter in-house and then the sample is sent out to factories for pricing **(E)**.

The mock-up is taken apart and the pieces are scanned to create digital patterns for die cutting. The final artwork is created, digitally or by hand, from illustration to engineering. The artwork is then sent to the factory **(F)**.

At the factory, the parts are laid out like a puzzle and fit onto a nesting sheet that contains all of the printed pieces that will be cut out.

The parts are printed and then the printed sheets are die cut: Lasers are used to cut grooves into large wooden boards (similar in size to the printed sheets) and knife blades are inserted into the grooves. Sheets of paper are fed into the die cutter one sheet at a time, and the blades cut the paper into the parts for the card **(G)**.

Assembly! An industrial designer plans the flow of the assembly, often employing fifty to seventy-five people to produce a complex pop-up book. Each person in the assembly line is responsible for assembling one part of the card or book **(H)**.

All images courtesy of Up With Paper

Basic Tools and Materials

PAPER

Basic card stock from the office supply store will work for most projects, and once you get the hang of making pop-ups, you will want to experiment with other papers and develop your own style. You might need a particular thickness for rigidity or a texture that allows the paper to slip and slide. For reference, I have included the type of paper used for each project in the book. There are often two steps to making pop-ups: practicing on a model and then making the real thing. Models can even be constructed with inexpensive office paper; once you determine your structural needs, a more appropriate paper can be picked out.

These are assorted card stocks available through Discount Card Stock (see Resources, page 143).

There are a few qualities that you should consider when choosing paper:

PAPER GRAIN

Have you ever folded a sheet of paper in half and noticed that the folded edge cracks? This is what happens when paper is folded against the grain. When manufactured commercially, paper fibers align in the direction that the fibers flow on the machine. When you buy sheets of paper, they have been cut down from larger sheets or rolls. In general, the longer dimension indicates the grain direction (for example, the grain on a 22 × 40-inch [56 × 101.6 cm] sheet runs in the 40-inch [101.6 cm] direction.)

PAPER THICKNESS/WEIGHT

Papers come in a variety of weights commonly referred to as text weight (normal office copier paper) or cover weight (card stock and heavier). The thickness of a sheet of paper is often measured with calipers and is typically given in thousandths of an inch. The weight of a paper is described using a complex system in pounds in the United States and grams per square meter in Europe. Card stocks ranging from 65 lb. to 110 lb. work well for most pop-up projects.

THE LONGEVITY OF PAPER

If you are making a work of art that you want to last longer than your lifetime, you will want to use an acid-free paper. Some papers are inherently acid-free due to their content (100 percent cotton rag paper, for example) and others are treated to make them pH neutral. Most paper suppliers offer information about the content of the papers they carry.

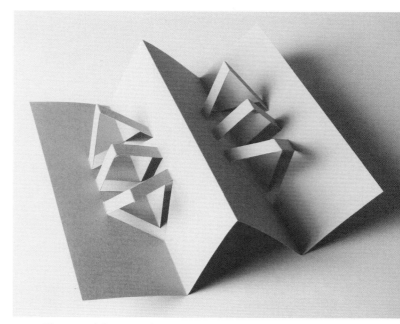

The grain of the paper should be taken into account, especially if all of the folds in a project occur parallel to each other.

DECORATING PAPER

Most pop-up books we see are printed commercially in full color by the thousands. When you make your own pop-ups, you need to consider how they will be illustrated. Throughout this book, you will see many illustration styles, ranging from the simplicity of pure white paper to digital art and collage. Use these as inspiration or embellish your projects in your own unique style. The sky is the limit!

Basic Tools and Materials

Here is a guide to special tools and materials for working with pop-ups.

Knives and mats: Most of the projects in this book require a craft knife **(A)**. My favorite type is the one that takes a #11 blade. Replace the blade often; as with knives in the kitchen, a sharp knife makes cutting easier, especially on thicker papers. A cutting mat **(B)** protects your work surface and keeps the knife blade from getting dull; most have grids printed on them, which makes it easy to measure and cut straight lines.

Cutting tools: I have a small paper cutter in my studio for cutting small sheets to size, as well as an assortment of scissors **(C)**. (I rarely use scissors, and when I do it's usually just for rough cutting and cutting curved lines that I can reach with them. I use my craft knife for all interior cuts as well as for straight lines). When you need to cut perfect circles, use a circle cutter **(D)**. This tool requires a steady hand and frequent blade changes and must be used on a cutting mat.

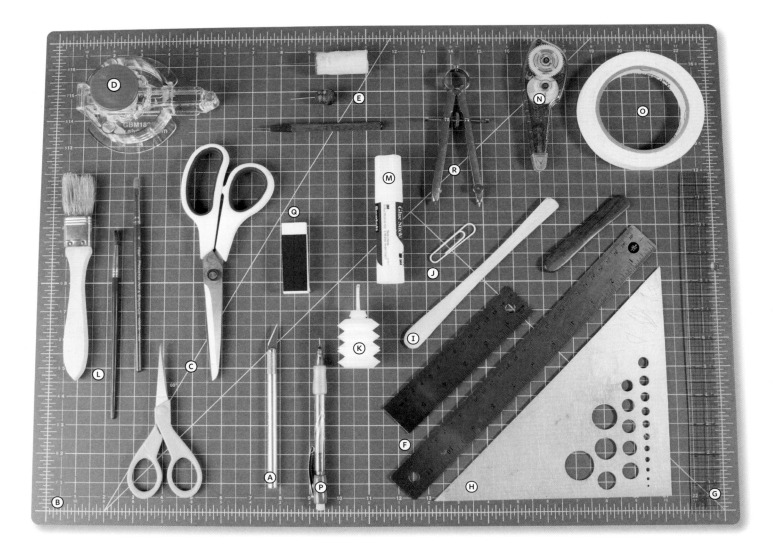

CUTTING MULTIPLE SHEETS OF PAPER

If you get into cutting multiple pop-ups in which you are repeatedly cutting the same thing over and over, you might want to consider purchasing a plotter cutter or vinyl cutter (often used in the sign industry). These electronic cutting machines cut from digital files and make producing multiples much faster and less labor intensive. If you decide to send your work out to be produced, it might be laser cut or die cut.

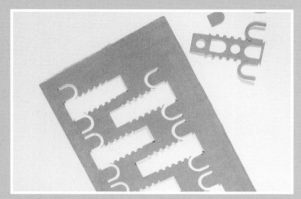

Laser-cut paper

Piercing tools: An awl or a potter's needle (make your own by poking a needle into a cork) works well for punching holes or for marking points to cut between when cutting lots of slots **(E)**.

Triangles and straightedges: I prefer a metal ruler **(F)** or straightedge for cutting because a plastic ruler **(G)** can fray when running a knife along its edge. I have rulers ranging in length from 6 to 36 inches (15.2 to 91.4 cm), and I use the size that best fits the project. Many metal rulers have cork on the back, which keeps them from slipping when cutting and scoring. I like a transparent plastic graph ruler for measuring because it has a grid of lines on it, which makes plotting and drawing parallel lines easy. A metal triangle comes in handy when plotting and cutting angles **(H)**.

Folding and scoring tools: A bone folder **(I)** is a common bookbinding tool used to score paper in preparation for folding as well as for creasing folds. They are typically made from bone (cow or deer), but some are made from wood, plastic, or even Teflon. In a pinch, you can use the back of a knife or a paper clip **(J)** as a scoring tool. It is helpful to place the paper you are scoring on a cutting mat or a few pieces of card stock to cushion the paper when scoring. Proper scoring is done on the side of the sheet that will be folded outward. For example, you score on the outside of a card. In some cases, cut-scoring (using a craft knife to cut halfway through the paper, especially on stiff card stock) makes folding more accurate and precise (see the Tower of Babel project on page 41).

Adhesives and applicators: My favorite adhesive is PVA glue, which is a white, clear-drying, archival glue, and I love using a mini glue applicator **(K)**, which is available from The Lamp Shop (see Resources, page 143). Brushes **(L)** also work. Glue sticks **(M)** are useful for temporary gluing and when gluing thin papers, such as tissue paper. Double-sided tape **(N)** is thin and works well for laminating sheets of paper together; artists' tape **(O)** is repositionable and doesn't leave residue, which makes it perfect for building models.

Drawing tools: Pencils **(P)** and erasers **(Q)** are essential for planning and marking your measurements. A divider and/or compass **(R)** can come in handy for measuring and drafting circles.

Techniques for Building Pop-Ups

There are a few basic techniques that will aid in the creation of pop-ups.

Cutting: Some pop-ups can be cut with scissors, but many require a craft knife, especially if interior cuts need to be made.

Folding and scoring: It is most common to score a sheet of paper (A) and then fold it away from the score (B). For example, a greeting card would be scored on the outside. For many of these projects, we will ignore this scoring rule because almost all pop-ups require mountain and valley folds (which would require scoring on both sides of the sheet). Instead, make all score lines on one side and then set the folds as needed.

Gluing: It is handy to have scrap paper available when gluing. Gluing out onto scrap paper ensures that the entire tab or piece of paper gets coated with glue. I often squirt glue onto my paper with an applicator and then smooth it out with a brush (C).

TRAINING YOUR POP-UPS

When gluing, take care to create an even, thin coat and try to avoid letting any glue squeeze out. Excess glue doesn't look good, and it can also hinder the functionality of a pop-up. Many pop-ups do not fold well the first time you fold them, especially complex mechanisms. Close the completed pop-up and carefully massage the folded mechanism to make small adjustments to the folds. Open and close your completed pop-ups a few times to train the folds so they learn how and when to move.

In many of the projects in the book, one side of a pop-up gets adhered to a base card. Then, the entire pop-up mechanism is collapsed flat, glue is applied to the glue tab, and by simply closing the card, the tab gets set in the correct place. Always open the folded card after gluing to make sure nothing sticks where it isn't supposed to be.

POP-UP WARM-UPS

Grab your cutting mat, a craft knife, and some glue or double-sided tape and create a few pop-up structures here in the pages of the book. They will become part of the pop-up vocabulary that you can refer back to as you create the projects in the book and go on to engineer your own creations. Don't forget to check out the great information on making pop-ups in the Resources section at the back of the book, too. Once you become familiar with the basic techniques, feel free to experiment and adapt them to create your own pop-ups. The possibilities are virtually endless.

Refer to the Symbol Key below when creating the pop-up warm-ups beginning on page 24. The key tells you which lines to cut, which lines to fold, and where to glue. Remember that mountain folds look like mountains, and valley folds look like valleys.

SYMBOL KEY

————————	Cut
- - - - - - - -	Mountain fold
· · · · · · · · · · · ·	Valley fold

1 . . . 2 . . . 3 . . . SLITS

Working your way from the top to the bottom of this page, create a simple pop-up by just cutting one slit in the sheet, progress to two parallel slits, and finally try your hand at a multiple-slit pop-up.

INSTRUCTIONS

STEP 1: CUT

Slip a cutting mat between pages 26 and 27. Using a straight-edge, cut along all of the solid lines. Alternatively, you can make the scores first, and then fold the center vertical fold and cut the slits through both layers of the paper at once.

STEP 2: SCORE

Score along all of the dotted lines.

STEP 3: FOLD AND POP

I find it helpful to fold the center vertical fold before making the folds for the pop-ups. Fold the pop-ups back and forth along the score lines and then open the spread and use the Symbol Key on page 23 to determine which folds are mountains and which are valleys.

VARIATIONS

....

1. Make the slit shorter or longer to create various triangle shapes.
2. Vary the angle of the cut line.

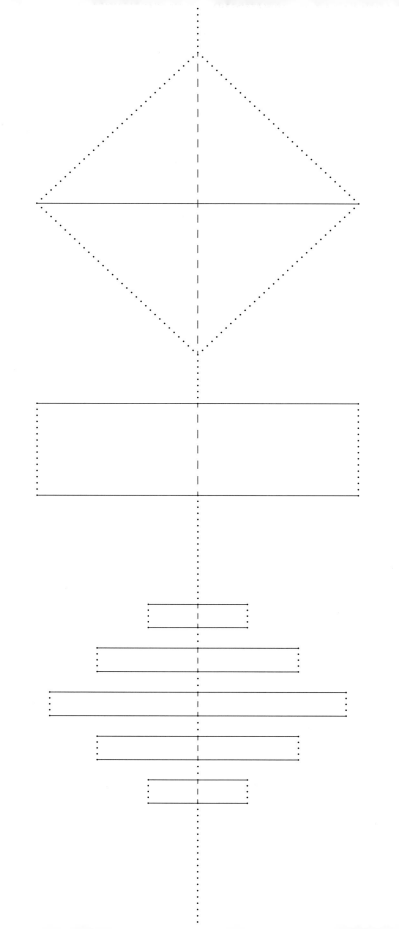

THREE P'S: Parallelogram, Pop-on-Pop, and Pop-in-Pop

Try these slightly more advanced mechanisms to make a parallelogram; cut secondary pop-ups out of the valleys formed by a central pop-up; and cut pop-ups within other pop-ups.

INSTRUCTIONS

STEP 1: CUT AND SCORE
Place your cutting mat between pages 30 and 31 and cut along all of the solid lines. Score along the dotted lines.

STEP 2: FOLD
Carefully push the pop-ups into place and crease the folds using the picture and the Symbol Key on page 23 as guides for mountain and valley folds. Take care not to fold the central fold on the parallelogram.

NOTE: Every pop-up spans a central fold. On the previous pop-up, the elements on each side of the fold are equal and symmetrical. With the parallelogram, you will discover how to work asymmetrically. Duncan Birmingham eloquently explains the basic foundation shapes found in pop-ups as well as the geometry behind them in his book *Pop-Up Design and Paper Mechanics* (see Resources, page 143).

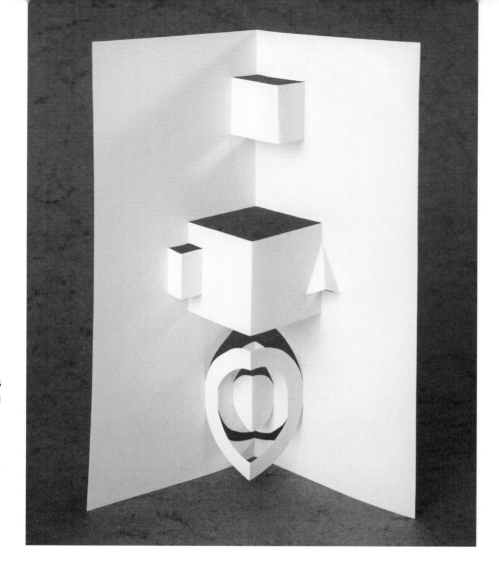

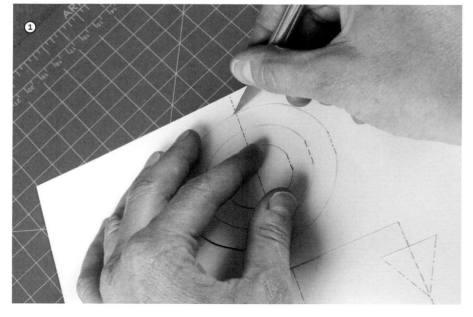

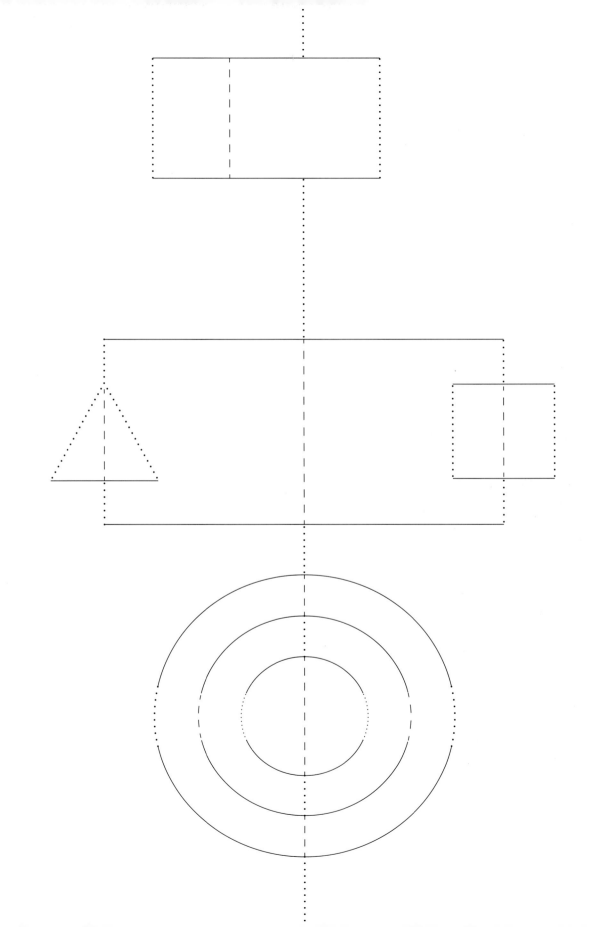

V-FOLDS AND DIVING DIAMONDS

Up until now, we've just cut and folded a single sheet of paper, but a majority of pop-ups are created by adding elements that are cut out and glued onto or on either side of the central spine with tabs.

You will have to cut the diamond pop-up at the bottom of the page to experience how it works because a photograph just cannot illustrate how the diamonds dive and flip as the page is folded and unfolded.

INSTRUCTIONS

STEP 1: CUT
Place your mat between pages 34 and 35. Cut along all of the solid lines of the rectangular shape and remove it from the page. Fold the page in half prior to cutting the solid lines on the diamond shape—you will be cutting through two layers of paper, but this will make the cuts and folds more accurate.

STEP 2: SCORE
Score along all of the dotted lines, including the dotted lines on the rectangle that you cut out.

STEP 3: FOLD
With the page still folded in half, fold the doubled sheet along the score lines in both directions to reinforce the folds of the diamond. Unfold the entire page and carefully push

the pop-ups into place using the picture and the Symbol Key on page 23 as guides for mountain and valley folds. Crease the folds and fold the page in half, massaging the folds into place. Fold and unfold the page and watch the diamonds flip!

STEP 4: GLUE
Fold the rectangular piece as indicated and glue the two tabs onto the center line as shown in the photo above.

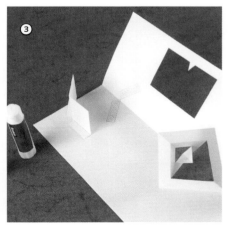

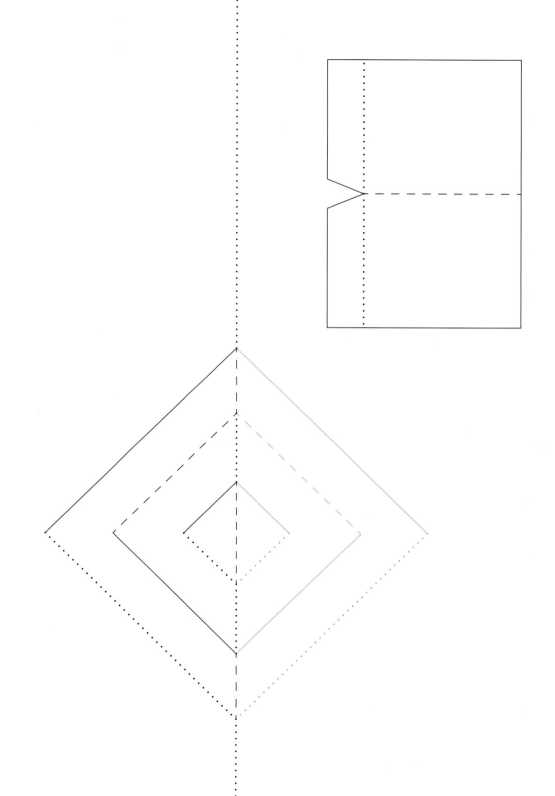

CHAPTER 2

Projects to Play With: Artistic Ideas for Popping, Engineering & Moving Paper

Explore the following fifteen pop-up projects, designed by some of today's top paper engineers. Each one is unique and shows the versatility of paper. Follow their instructions and learn how to cut, fold, and pop paper in ways you've never imagined. Once you've worked your way through this set of projects, you'll have a greater understanding of how you can make paper move between two and three dimensions. I hope you will be inspired to create your own movables and that you will come up with new techniques for playing with pop-ups!

Projects at left (top to bottom; left to right): *Bloodroot Plant*, Shawn Sheehy; *Pop-Up Accordion Book*, Dorothy A. Yule; *Carousel Pop-Up Book*, Emily Martin; *Puppy Puppet*, Mary Beth Cryan

① ② ③ ④

VARIATIONS

Play around with the cuts and folds. Try cutting a circle or a square as the main shape and then cut into it using various angles. You could even try using deckled-edged scissors.

Pop-Up Paper Earrings

These earrings may not be the most practical form of jewelry, but if you use sturdy paper and are careful, they are sure to hold up for several occasions, if not longer. And, because they take no time to make, try altering and experimenting with various cuts, folds, and papers to make several pairs in one sitting. Perhaps you'll come up with a design you love so much that you will have a more permanent version fabricated in metal one day.

INSTRUCTIONS

STEP 1: CUT AND FOLD
Download the earring pattern (or enlarge and photocopy the template on page 120 twice) and print them onto the back side of a sheet of card stock. Cut out the two 1½" (3.8 cm) squares. Orient one square so that it looks like a diamond and fold it in half, point to point, creating an equilateral triangle. Repeat for the second earring.

STEP 2: CUT, SCORE, AND FOLD
Cut the tip off the top of one of the triangles along the solid line. Cut through both layers of the triangle along the four lines that run parallel to the sides of the triangle, ending at the dotted lines.Using the scoring tool, score along the two fold lines as indicated in the diagram. Fold the paper back and forth along those two lines.

STEP 3: POP UP
Unfold the square of paper and pop the larger diamond shape out and then push the inner diamond shape in to create the pop-up. Repeat for the second earring.

STEP 4: ATTACH EARRING PARTS
Attaching the paper to the earring will depend on the type of earring parts that you acquire. I used these two different methods:
A. Place a small dab of glue on the straight end of an eye pin (first cut the pin to the desired length using wire cutters) and glue it to the center fold of the paper. Next, pry open the eye and slip it onto the ear wire.

B. Pierce a small hole in the paper with a needle, potter's needle, or awl and thread a single wire loop through it. Connect a pinch bail earring hook and ear wire assembly to the loop.

MATERIALS

earring template (see page 120)
decorative card stock
craft knife
cutting mat
straightedge
scoring tool
triangle (optional)
pencil
earring findings

CONSIDERATIONS

Jewelry findings are surprisingly easy to find. You can locate these items in craft stores, jewelry shops, hobby shops, and online. Or, if you work with metal or know a jeweler, you can have something custom made with finer materials.

PAPER ENGINEER: Helen Hiebert
POP-UP MECHANISM/STYLE: origamic architecture
PAPER: Unbuffered bond paper (available from Talas). Note: This paper was used to enhance the marbling process.
ILLUSTRATION STYLE: hand marbled by Steve Pittelkow

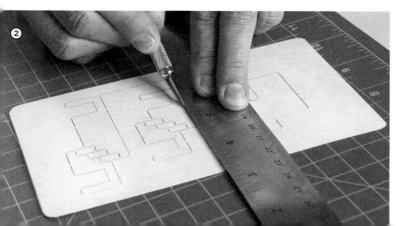

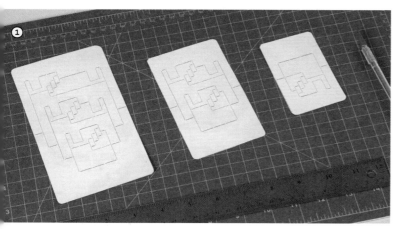

Tower of Babel

Paper engineer Elod Beregszaszi is a master of origamic architecture, a form of pop-ups that involves cutting, scoring, and folding a single sheet of paper, often without removing any parts, to create three-dimensional forms. Beregszaszi created this Tower of Babel, representing the Bible story in which the people of the earth decided to build a city with a tower that would reach heaven. He has designed it in stages, beginning with a simple one-story building and progressing up to three stories. Once you get the hang of the construction, you'll be able to build your own tower that reaches the sky.

INSTRUCTIONS

STEP 1: PREP AND CUT

Download the patterns (or enlarge and photocopy the templates on page 120) and print them onto the back side of a sheet of card stock. Use scissors or a craft knife and straightedge to cut out the three versions of the tower. Use a craft knife and straightedge to cut along the solid lines that appear in the interior of each tower.

STEP 2: CUT-SCORE

Instead of scoring, use a straightedge and craft knife to carefully cut-score along all of the dotted and dashed lines, breaking through the paper's surface but not cutting all the way through it. This form of scoring is precise and makes the folding easier.

STEP 3: FOLD

This takes a bit of practice with the tiny cuts and folds, but most papers are forgiving. Start popping the parts of the building out from the side that the markings are on (these will remain on the back of your tower, thus being hidden). Carefully crease the longer horizontal mountain and valley folds while pushing the more intricate pieces, such as the stairs, into position. Use a craft knife or scoring tool to assist in popping the smaller pieces into place. When all of the folds are set, collapse the entire card and press along the folds to reinforce them.

MATERIALS

· · · · · · · · · · · · · · · · · · · ·

Tower of Babel templates
  (see page 120)
card stock
straightedge
cutting mat
craft knife
scissors (optional)

NOTE

· · · · · · · · · · · · · · · · · · · ·

These are three separate projects: There is a version with just one floor, a two-story version, and a tower with three levels. Start with the one-floor version to get the hang of it and then progress to two and three stories.

PAPER ENGINEER: Elod Beregszaszi
POP-UP MECHANISM/STYLE: origamic architecture
PAPER: off-white card stock
ILLUSTRATION STYLE: none

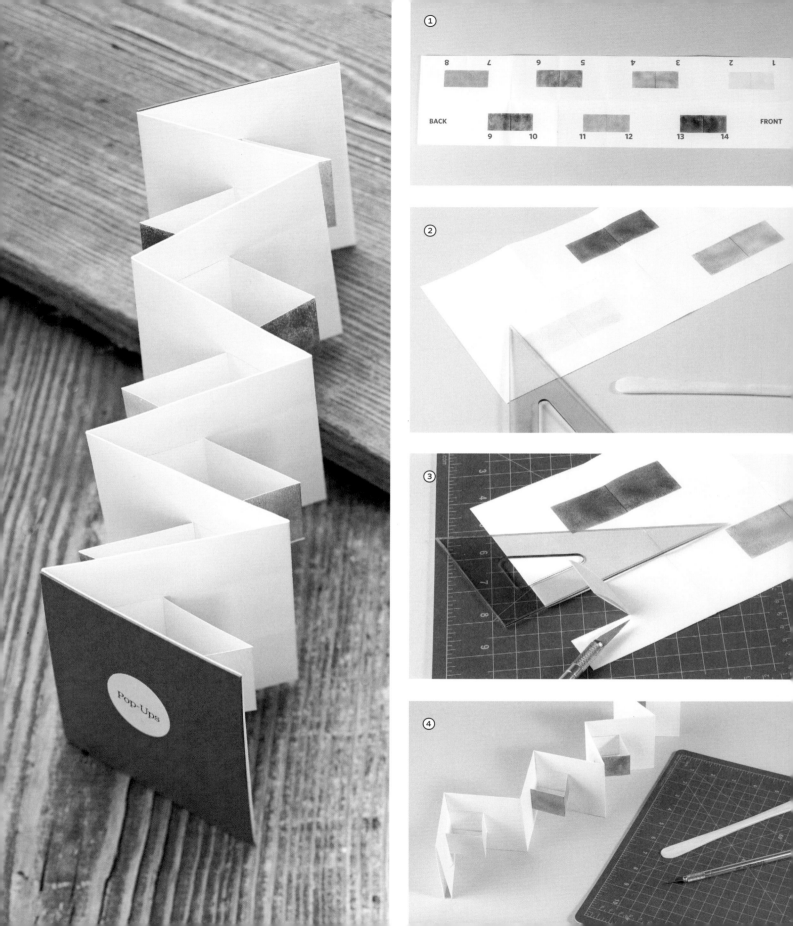

8 7 6 5 4 3 2 1

BACK

9 10 11 12 13 14

FRONT

②

③

④

Pop-Up Accordion Book

Dorothy Yule developed this clever structure for her two miniature pop-up books: *Souvenir of New York* and *Souvenir of San Francisco*. By using a double layer of paper, she created a way to make pop-ups on both sides of an accordion fold, without seeing through from one side to the other. This allows the content of the book to be twice as long and the pop-ups twice as many! When you finish reading one side of the book, you can turn the book over and keep reading.

INSTRUCTIONS

See "Folding an Accordion," page 44. Fold the paper in half lengthwise. Unfold it and fold it in half widthwise. Then fold an eight-section accordion using a scoring tool to reinforce each fold. Reverse all of the accordion folds (unfold and refold them in the other direction; use a scoring tool to reinforce the folds).

STEP 1: CREATE THE FIRST POP-UP

Unfold the paper again to its full size. The diagram, or *imposition*—in printing terms, this refers to the arrangement of a printed product's pages—indicates the page numbers so that you can lay out your book accordingly. (See the labels added to photograph 1; mark yours lightly in pencil.) This is important if your book has a story line or needs to be viewed in a certain order.

STEP 2: DRAW AND SCORE

Beginning on spread one/two, draw a simple rectangular pop-up panel that is centered on the middle fold and is not wider than half the width of each panel (otherwise the pop-up will stick out when the pages are folded). Using a triangle and a scoring tool, score along the two short edges of the rectangle that are parallel to the center fold.

STEP 3: CUT AND FOLD

Next, reverse the fold that lies between pages one and two, and using a craft knife or scissors, cut through the two layers of paper along the top and bottom edges of the rectangle. Fold and crease the sides of the rectangle along the score lines so that the rectangle pops up.

STEP 4: REPEAT AND ASSEMBLE

Repeat step 2 on each fold ($3/4$, $5/6$, $7/8$, $9/10$, $11/12$, $13/14$). When complete, refold the accordion book structure and carefully pull each rectangle forward, reversing the folds at each side to form the pop-ups.

MATERIALS

80 lb. text weight paper cut to $6\frac{1}{4}" \times 25"$ (16 × 63.5 cm), with the grain running in the $6\frac{1}{4}"$ (16 cm) direction

heavy card stock or box board

craft knife

cutting mat

ruler

scoring tool

triangle

pencil

PVA glue

glue brush

CONSIDERATIONS

You can create the imagery for the pop-ups in this book using any means you like: drawing, transferring, collage, etc. Dorothy Yule used an old stenciling technique called *pochoir* to create the colored shapes.

FOLDING AN ACCORDION

Take these simple steps to fold a perfect accordion, but first, make sure the paper's grain runs in the direction of the accordion folds:

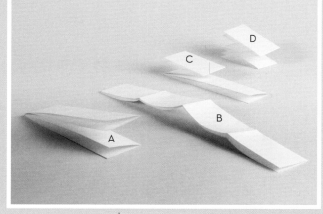

1. Place the sheet of paper on the work surface and fold it in half, matching up the short edges as perfectly as possible. Turn the folded paper to position the folded edge at the top of the work surface (A).

2. Take the top leaf (here, a double layer because the paper is already folded in half) of paper and fold it up, matching it up with the top folded edge. Crease the fold. Flip the paper over and repeat with the top leaf of paper on the other side. There are now four layers of paper.

3. Unfold the paper gently and set it on your work surface so that there is a valley fold (when unfolded, the fold looks like the letter "V," or a valley) in between two mountain folds (when unfolded, the fold looks like a mountain ridge). Reverse the valley fold so that there are three mountain folds (B). Now fold the top mountain fold up to meet the single leaf edge of the sheet, aligning the edges and creasing the new fold (C). Fold the middle and last folds up in the same manner, aligning all of the edges and creasing each fold. Finally, fold the bottom leaf up to complete an accordion which is half the size of the original (D). There are now eight sections.

STEP 5: MAKE COVERS

Cut two pieces of heavy card stock or box board to the width and height of the book. Place one of the covers facedown on a piece of scrap paper and apply glue to the entire inside of the cover. Remove the scrap paper and press the cover onto the front of the accordion. Repeat with the back cover.

VARIATIONS

1. Change the shape of the pop-ups by changing the shape of the parallel cuts—you can create pop-up circles, hexagons, triangles, and other shapes.

2. Create a silhouette in the shape of an image.

3. Cut a secondary pop-up out of the valley formed by the central pop-up: Use a craft knife to cut parallel lines to form two small rectangular shapes that span the valley folds of the central pop-up. Score along the vertical sides on each side of the valley fold. Gently pop the rectangles out from the page, folding and creasing along the vertical score lines.

4. Glue shapes or images onto the central pop-ups.

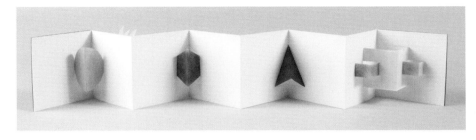

PAPER ENGINEER: Dorothy Yule

POP-UP MECHANISM/STYLE: Double-sided accordion with simple pop-ups

PAPER: 80 lb. Mohawk Superfine text weight (accordion); Conservation by Design premier sepia-colored box board (cover)

ILLUSTRATION STYLE: Pochoir stenciling

Pop-Up City Skyline

Author and book artist Paul Johnson has devised numerous lightweight collapsible structures by studying cellular packaging structures. His pop-up books utilize interlocking slots and tabs (sometimes referred to as *slice forms*) that allow them to collapse flat. Use this clever technique to create a pop-up skyline of your favorite city!

Warm-Up Exercise

Here's an easy way to make a four-cell grid. Try it first to learn the ropes and then move on to the city skyline. Use a lightweight card stock or heavy text paper for this structure because you'll be folding it several times. Once you've mastered the technique, you can also try using stiffer papers or even cardboard to make more durable cell structures.

INSTRUCTIONS

STEP 1: FOLD
Fold a sheet of 8½" × 11" (21.6 × 28 cm) paper in half the short way. Now fold the folded sheet in half again, in the other direction.

MATERIALS
....

8½" × 11" (21.6 × 28 cm)
   lightweight card stock
straightedge
triangle
craft knife or scissors
cutting mat (optional)

①

Paper Engineer: Paul Johnson
Pop-Up Mechanism/Style: slice form
Paper: watercolor paper (90 lb. for the cell structure and 140 lb. for the base)
Illustration Style: dampened with cold water and then painted with fabric dyes

STEP 2: MORE FOLDING

Fold the top and bottom edges to the middle crease and then refold the middle crease, creating a *W* shape.

STEP 3: MEASURE AND CUT

Using a ruler, mark points along the folded edges (the bottom of the *W*) at ½", 2¾", and 5" (1.3, 7, and 12.7 cm). Use the triangle to draw three perpendicular lines beginning at the markings and running to the middle of the strip. Cut along these lines using a craft knife or scissors. Make sure you cut through all of the layers.

STEP 4: UNFOLD AND CUT STRIPS

Unfold the entire sheet of paper and cut along all of the creases (scissors are fine, but a craft knife and straightedge will yield more accurate cuts). You will have eight strips, but you only need six to create the structure.

STEP 5: INTERLOCK

Interlock the slits to create a four-cell structure.

City Skyline

INSTRUCTIONS

STEP 1: PREPARE THE TEMPLATES
Download the patterns (or enlarge and photocopy the templates on pages 121–122) and print them onto card stock.

STEP 2: CUT OUT SKYLINE
Use a craft knife and a ruler to cut out the three skyline pieces. Cut the two slits on each piece. Illustrate the buildings as desired. (There is no need to complete in detail the bottom areas of the back two pieces because these will be hidden from view.)

STEP 3: CUT OUT BRACKETS
Cut two 2" × 4" (5 × 10.2 cm) pieces out of another sheet of paper. Illustrate both sides of the brackets as desired. Measure and cut three slits on each strip: The slits should be 1" (2.5 cm) apart and 1" (2.5 cm) long, so that they are cut halfway through each bracket.

STEP 4: ASSEMBLE
Interlock the three layers with the brackets. After interlocking all of the pieces, collapse the entire piece sideways and fold it down flat. Just lift the edges to open it again.

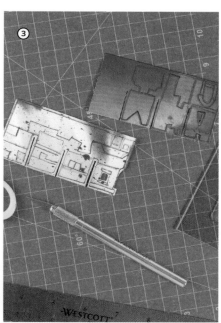

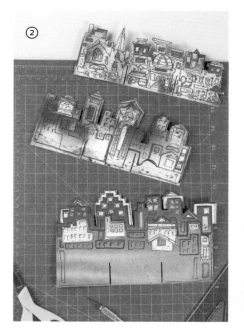

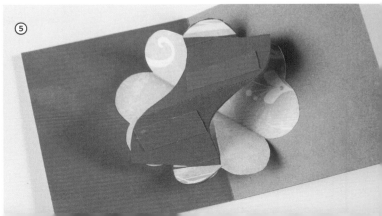

Pop-Up Valentine

Surprise your sweetheart with this clever pop-up, engineered by Kyle Olmon. This project combines two basic building blocks of paper engineering (the *V-fold* and the *box layer*) into one dynamic pop-up mechanism that twists when opened. Enjoy picking out papers and coming up with your own clever inscription to make valentines for your friends and loved ones.

Pop-Up Terminology

There is no true codified lexicon for the mechanisms used in paper engineering. For instance, this twister can also go by the name *transformer*, which refers to when a window is cut out of the cover to reveal a transformation from one image to another as the card is opened, or it can be referred to as *opposing angles with a tent*. The important thing to remember is that you should stack a square box layer over two opposing right-angle V-folds of equal size for this pop-up to operate properly. You can also use other variations, such as circles or tall rectangles, instead of the diagonal scroll piece to create your pop-up card.

PAPER ENGINEER: Kyle Olmon
POP-UP MECHANISM/STYLE: box layer, V-folds, and twister
PAPER: colored card stocks
ILLUSTRATION STYLE: collage

INSTRUCTIONS

STEP 1: PREPARE THE TEMPLATE
Download the patterns (or enlarge and photocopy the templates on page 123) and print them onto appropriately colored card stocks. Add any decoration.

STEP 2: SCORE, FOLD, AND CUT
Using a straightedge as a guide, score along all of the lines that indicate folds in the pop-up pieces and the base card. Carefully cut out the pop-up pieces and the card base along the solid black lines. Fold along all of the scored lines. The dashes indicate mountain folds and the dots indicate valley folds.

STEP 3: GLUE THE HEART ONTO BASE
Apply a thin layer of glue to the two shaded areas on the base card. Place the unfolded hearts on the pop-up piece over the glued areas, making sure that the creases on the two folded hearts are directly on top of the crease in the base card. Carefully fold the card to make sure everything is set in the right place and let the glue dry.

STEP 4: GLUE SCROLL
Apply a dab of glue to the back of the two folded tabs on the top and bottom of the scroll pop-up piece. Attach these two ends of the scroll piece to the heart piece, aligning the curves on the tabs with the top-right and bottom-left curves on the folded hearts.

STEP 5: GLUE CURVED PIECES
Glue the small curved pieces onto the ends of the heart/scroll. After allowing the glue to dry, carefully close the card while making sure everything folds properly, and you are done!

MATERIALS

valentine templates (see page 123)
two or three complementary
   card stock papers
straightedge
scoring tool
scissors
white glue or glue stick
glue brush (optional)

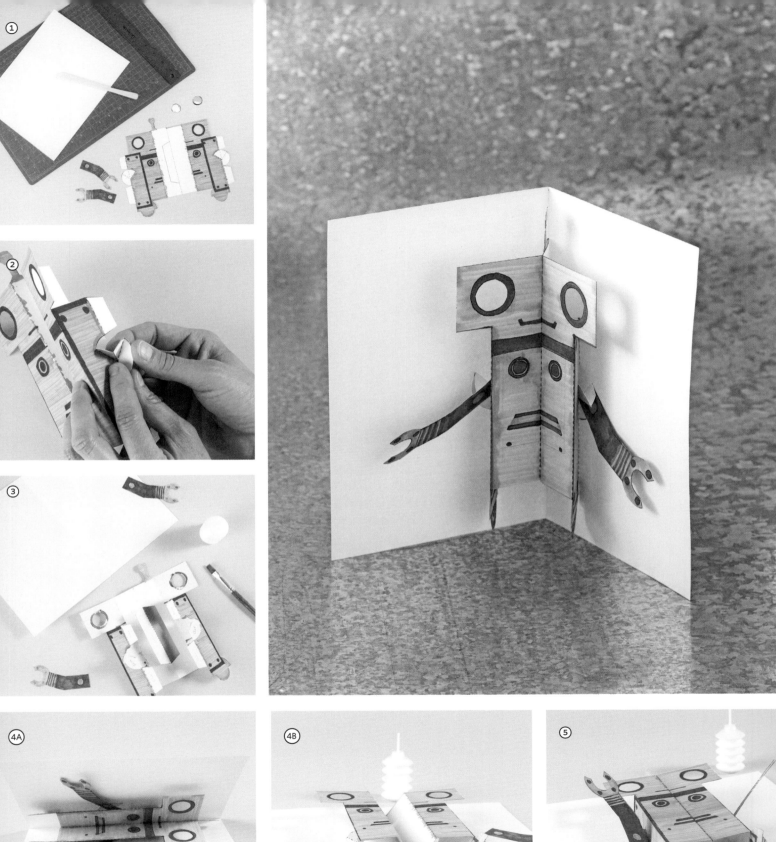

Pop-Up Robot

This little guy looks like he could do some work with his wrench-like hands. Paper engineer Sam Ita designed this clever robot whose body is made from a single piece of paper. He flaps his arms as the page opens and looks like he might want a hug. Hmmm, what *is* our world coming to?

INSTRUCTIONS

STEP 1: CUT AND SCORE
Download the pattern sheets (or enlarge and photocopy the templates on page 123) and print them onto card stock. Cut out the robot assemblage, cut the arms into two pieces, and score along all of the lines indicating folds. Cut along all solid lines in the interior of the robot body (the eyes, the tab in the center, the slits below the eyes, and the inner part of the circles on the sides). Score the center fold of the second piece of card stock and fold it in half to make a base for the robot.

STEP 2: FOLD ROBOT BODY
Follow the key and fold along the lines: Dots indicate valley folds and dashes indicate mountain folds. Valley-fold the robot's body in half; the central tab can be folded either way. Mountain-fold the rest of the panels and tabs that are parallel to the center panels. Valley-fold the central vertical lines that mark

the diameter of the circular arm tabs. Place a finger behind the top of one arm tab and gently push it forward, creating a V-fold on the three triangular section score lines. Pinch the V-fold flat to reinforce the folds. Repeat on the other arm tab.

STEP 3: COLLAPSE THE ROBOT
Turn the robot over, fold the sides in, and collapse the robot body flat, making sure that all of the tabs are showing and that the circular arm tabs are folded as well.

STEP 4: GLUE THE ROBOT
A. Apply glue to the two arm tabs, the four body tabs, and the central tab. Flip the body over carefully and center it vertically in the crease of the base, firmly pressing in the glued areas to adhere them.
B. Apply glue to the center body panels and adhere them to each other.

STEP 5: ATTACH THE ARMS
Apply glue to the forward-facing triangle on one of the arm tabs and attach the appropriate arm, pushing the end of the arm up against the robot's body. Repeat with the other arm. Your robot is ready to move!

PAPER ENGINEER: Sam Ita
POP-UP MECHANISM/STYLE: Main body is unsecured box; arms powered by V-folds
PAPER: 67 lb. white card stock
ILLUSTRATION STYLE: rendered with Copic watercolor markers by Aimee Ita

MATERIALS
....

robot templates (see
   page 123)
2 sheets of 8½" × 11"
   (21.6 × 28 cm) white
   card stock
craft knife
scissors (optional)
cutting mat (optional)
straightedge
scoring tool
markers (optional)
white glue
glue brush

Bloodroot Plant

Bloodroot (Sanguinaria canadensis), gets its name from the bright red dye that can be made from the plant's root. Shawn Sheehy developed this project for a workshop series he teaches at botanic gardens, and bloodroot is also one of twelve pop-up flowers featured in his artist's book *Pop-Up Guide to Wildflowers.* Shawn calls this a "butterfly structure" because it makes the motion of a butterfly when opening and closing. As a result, it's a great structure to adapt and use for any flapping creature, such as a bird or a dragonfly.

INSTRUCTIONS

STEP 1: PREP AND CUT

Download the patterns (or enlarge and photocopy the templates on page 124) and print them onto the back side of appropriately colored card stocks. Cut out the flower and leaf pieces using sharp scissors or a cutting knife, taking care to cut right on the line (note that the printed tabs and lines appear on the back of the flower, so they will not show on the finished piece). Cut the base card (or folio) to 6¼" × 9" (16 × 23 cm), making sure that the grain is running in the 6¼" (16 cm) direction.

STEP 2: SCORE AND FOLD

Folio: Score the folio in the middle and fold it in half.
Leaves: Score and mountain-fold tabs C and D; score and valley-fold tabs E and F.

STEP 3: GLUE FLOWERS ONTO LEAVES AND INTERLOCK

Glue tab B of the flower to the back side of the leaf, as indicated on the pattern (orient the tab so that the B is visible, or faceup, after gluing). Repeat with tab A, gluing it to the other half of the leaf. Carefully slide the two halves of the flower together and interlock tabs E and F (hiding the tabs behind the leaves).

STEP 4: GLUE BLOODROOT ONTO CARD

Note: This structure features a parallel fold and therefore, the tab on the flower that glues to the base is parallel to the gutter. The structure is flexible in terms of where the leaves are glued onto the folio: The distance between the gutter and the glue guide can vary, depending on whether you want the flower to pop up or lie flat when the card is opened at a 180-degree angle.

Glue tabs C and D to the matching marks on the folio. Press firmly to make sure the glue adheres, and then carefully open and fold the card to make sure everything moves correctly. Let the glue dry. The flower will pop up a bit when the folio is opened at 180 degrees.

MATERIALS

bloodroot templates
 (see page 124)
three complementary
 card stock papers
pencil (optional)
straightedge
scoring tool
cutting mat
craft knife
white glue or glue stick
glue brush (optional)

Paper Engineer: Shawn Sheehy
Pop-Up Mechanism/Style: parallel fold with interlocking planes
Paper: 110 lb. card stock
Illustration Style: assorted colored papers

Pop-Up Dragon

What would you do if you opened a book page and saw a fire-breathing dragon? This pop-up, designed by Bruce Foster, has a story folded into it that comes alive each time you open the card. The V-folds incorporated into this structure allow the dragon to hide when the page is closed and extend beyond the page as it opens.

INSTRUCTIONS

STEP 1: SCORE

Download the pattern sheets (or enlarge and photocopy the templates on page 126) and print them onto card stock: print the two full-color sheets back-to-back on one sheet. Score along all of the lines for folds on the pop-up pieces. Score the center fold of the base card.

STEP 2: CUT OUT PARTS

This works best if you first separate each piece by cutting between the pieces (don't worry about cutting on the lines at this point). You will end up with six pieces. Then, carefully cut each piece along the colored edges with scissors.

MATERIALS

dragon templates (see page 126)

scissors

white glue

straightedge

scoring tool

scrap paper

STEP 3: FOLD THE DRAGON

Fold the dragon in half along the middle score line, creasing the fold sharply. Place your thumbnail along one of the dotted diagonal lines and press from behind with the fingers on your other hand to create a valley fold. Repeat with the other diagonal. With your fingers behind the dragon's neck and your thumbs in front, force the neck to bend forward while the diagonal lines below bend back. Press flat.

STEP 4: FOLD THE WINGS

Place your thumbnail along the end of one of the diagonals near the wing and press from behind, forcing the wing forward. Repeat on the other wing. Carefully press everything flat to train the folds.

STEP 5: GLUE DRAGON TO CARD

Valley-fold the piece of card stock with the dragon haunches silhouetted on it. Turn the dragon over and apply glue to the back of the haunches and tail. Apply glue to those two paper panels *only*. Carefully align the dragon's haunches along the central vertical fold on the card, attaching it to the shaded area. Press the dragon and the card flat, holding the haunches in place until the glue has set. Fold and unfold the card to make sure it functions properly.

PAPER ENGINEER: Bruce Foster
POP-UP MECHANISM: V-fold
PAPER: 65 lb. white card stock
ILLUSTRATION STYLE: Digital art

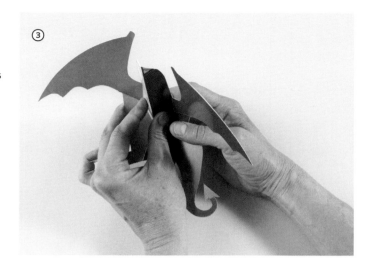

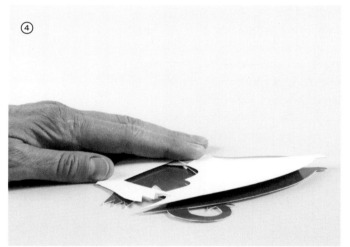

STEP 6: ATTACH THE ARMS

Glue the dragon's arms to spots A and B so that the diagonals on the dragon are flush with the diagonals of the arms.

STEP 7: ASSEMBLE THE HEAD

Pinch the triangle at the top of the neck, creating two mountain folds and a central valley fold along the marked lines. Apply glue to the section marked "head and neck" on the dragon's body and attach the dragon's head piece, aligning the diagonals at the base of the neck. Note that the tip of the yellow triangle is visible and lies just above the dragon's lower mouth.

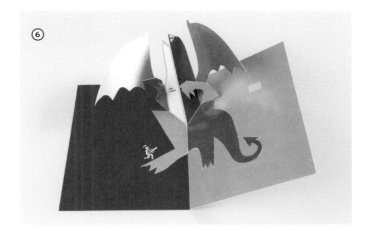

STEP 8: GLUE THE FLAME

Apply a small dab of glue to the triangle marked "flame" on the neck and attach the flame, orienting it so the triangles align. Press firmly in place.

STEP 9: ATTACH THE CASTLE

Apply a small dab of glue to the triangle tip (marked "B") on the princess tower and to the underside of the green tab at the tower's base. Slide the tip into the triangular wedge behind the dragon's right arm and press it into place. Make sure the base of the castle runs parallel to the top of the card and press the base tab in place. Fold the completed pop-up flat, testing the folds and reinforcing the glued pieces.

NOTE: Step 10 is only necessary if you were not able to print the base card back-to-back (i.e., if you have two pieces for the base card).

STEP 10: ATTACH THE BACK OF CARD

Mountain-fold the front of the card (with the knight printed on it). Lay this card facedown on a piece of scrap paper and apply glue to the entire back side of the card, gluing out over the edges onto the scrap paper. Carefully remove the scrap paper and discard it. Place the card with the dragon on it (make sure it is oriented properly) into the fold of the front of the card and firmly attach the two, making sure that the edges are perfectly aligned.

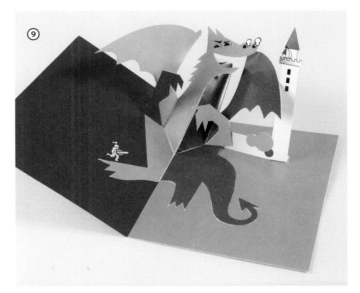

Pop-Up First Bank

Colette Fu makes artist's books that combine her photography with pop-up paper engineering. This is an image of the First Bank of the United States that she photographed in Philadelphia, where Alexander Hamilton developed a standardized form of currency. Once you make the First Bank, try rendering your own favorite buildings as three-dimensional pop-ups! This would be a clever way for architects to present building designs to clients, especially because they fold up flat and are portable—buildings on the go!

Terminology

This structure, when used with just one layer above the base layer, is called a *platform* or is sometimes referred to as a *floating platform*. This project features two layers in addition to the base layer, so we'll call it a *multi-layered platform*.

INSTRUCTIONS

STEP 1: PREP AND CUT

Download the patterns (or enlarge and photocopy the templates on page 128) and print them onto 8½" × 11" (21.6 × 28 cm) 110 lb. card stock or matte photo paper. Cut out the three buildings and two tabs using scissors. Cut out windows, doorways, and spacing between columns as desired.

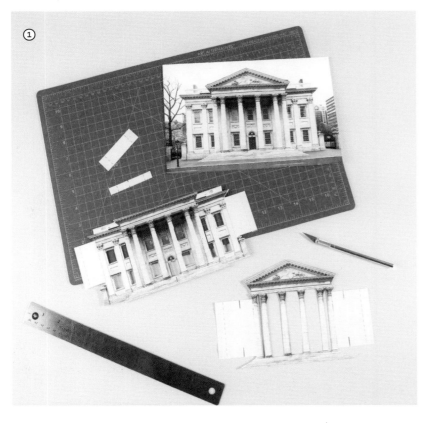

MATERIALS

three templates (see page 128)
scissors
craft knife
pencil
straightedge
white glue

VARIATIONS

When choosing your own images for this type of pop-up, good choices include symmetrical objects (a building), repetitive forms (bleachers), and layered images (organs of the body, as in those from old medical flap books). It is a good idea to use images in which all of the layers are flat and parallel to the background. Note that the greater number of platforms (this one has three), the narrower the distance between the layers must be so that everything stays within the background when the card is folded in half.

PAPER ENGINEER: Colette Fu
POP-UP MECHANISM: Multilayered platform
PAPER: 110 lb. card stock or matte photo paper
ILLUSTRATION STYLE: Digital art

STEP 2: CUT SLOTS

Use a craft knife to cut out the two large and two small slots on the bottom layer, two large and one small slot on the middle layer, four slits on the top layer, and two slits on the smaller loose tab. Note: Slots (within the sheet) and slits (cut in from the edge of the sheet) are indicated by white lines on the template. Make the slots thick enough to accommodate the paper thickness.

STEP 3: SCORE AND FOLD

Score along all lines for folds on the building parts and two loose tabs. Mountain-fold along these score lines, with all imagery facing up. In addition, score along the outer edges of the outermost columns on the top and middle layers and mountain-fold. Measure to the center lines and score the three building images in the middle. Valley-fold the three buildings in half.

STEP 4: ATTACH TABS TO TOP LAYER

Glue the larger tab to the back of the top layer just below the peak of the roof, aligning the tab flush with the fold of the building. Glue the smaller tab to the back of the top layer at the base of the building, aligning the tab with the fold of the building and orienting the tab so that the small slots are closest to the fold. Allow the glue to dry.

STEP 5: ASSEMBLE

A. Small tab on top layer: Carefully fold in the sides below the two slits so that you can thread it through the slot in the middle layer. Unfold the sides after threading to lock the tab in place. Slip the folded end of the tab into the bottom layer and glue it in place.

B. Large tab on top layer: Slip the folded end of the tab through the slot in the bottom layer and glue it in place.

C. Top layer outside edges: On each side, carefully fold in the sides below the two slits so that you can thread them through the middle layer. Thread each side through the middle layer, unfold the sides, and then slip the folded tab through the bottom layer and glue it in place.

D. Middle layer outside edges: Slip the folded tabs into the slots in the base layer and glue them in place on the back side of the base.

STEP 6: FOLD

Carefully open and fold the card to make sure everything moves correctly. Congratulations! You are a paper architect.

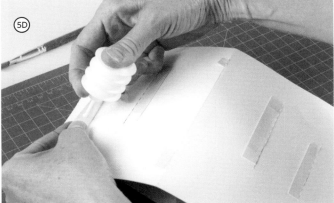

Pop-Up Tent and Pyramid

Pop-up wizard Carol Barton (author of three volumes of *The Pocket Paper Engineer*) still finds these dimensional pop-up forms magical. Just the idea that a three-dimensional pyramid and a tent could fold flat between a page spread invites a sense of wonder and a curiosity as to how it's done. Understanding the mechanics of the straddle pop-up used in the tent and the V-fold pop-up in the pyramid does not diminish the final effect. Your kiddos might have some mini figures who want to go camping or visit this pyramid!

TENT INSTRUCTIONS

(From the book *The Pocket Paper Engineer*, volume 2)

STEP 1: PREP AND CUT

Download the tent pattern (or enlarge and photocopy the templates on page 130) and cut it out along the outer solid black lines. Gently score and mountain-fold along the lines for folds (you will reverse some of these folds). Keep the pattern lines on the outside as you construct the tent so you can refer to them as you go.

NOTE

Remember that there are cut lines, valley-fold lines, mountain-fold lines, and areas to glue. Use the key on page 120 as your guide.

MATERIALS

....

templates (see page 130)
two sheets of 8½" × 11"
   (21.6 × 28 cm) card stock
scoring tool
metal ruler
scissors or craft knife
cutting mat
glue stick

STEP 2: GLUE
Glue both tabs marked 1 to the diagonally slashed areas marked 1 on the opposite flaps. This creates two triangular sides to the tent.

STEP 3: COLLAPSE THE TENT
Push the sides outward (mountain folds) to flatten the tent.

STEP 4: GLUE INTO BASE CARD
Fold the base card in half. Unfold it. Apply glue to tab 2 and position the scalloped edge of the glued tab along the fold of the left side of the card, centering it vertically.

STEP 5: PITCH THE TENT
Keeping the tent collapsed on the left side of the card, apply glue to tab 3 and fold the right side of the card down onto the tent, closing the card. Let the glue dry briefly. When you open it, the tent will pop up. Happy camping!

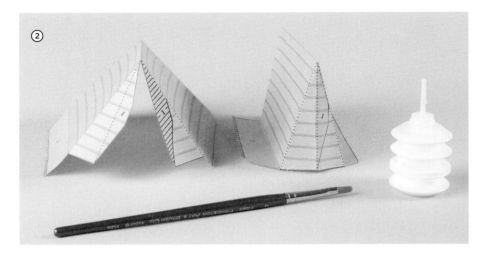

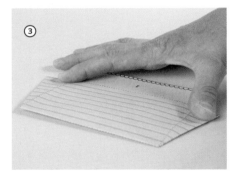

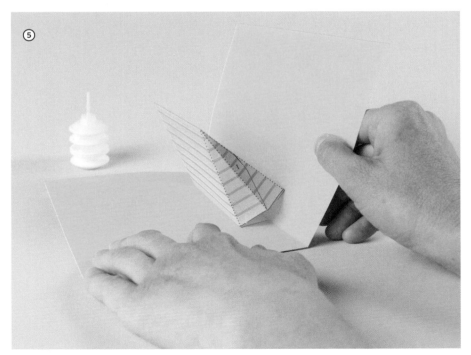

PAPER ENGINEER: Carol Barton

POP-UP MECHANISM: Leaning V-fold pop-up with a floating triangular back

PAPER: Pop-up is Passport text 70 lb. smooth; base card is Wausau Astrobrights 65 lb. card stock.

ILLUSTRATION STYLE: Computer generated

PYRAMID INSTRUCTIONS

(From the book *The Pocket Paper Engineer*, Volume 3)

STEP 1: PREP AND CUT

Download the pyramid pattern (or enlarge and photocopy the templates on page 131) and cut it out along the outer solid black lines. Gently score and mountain-fold along the dotted lines (you will reverse some of these folds). Keep the pattern lines on the outside as you construct the tent so you can refer to them as you work.

STEP 2: GLUE

Glue tab 1 to the diagonally slashed area marked 1 on the opposite flap. This creates a three-sided equilateral pyramid.

STEP 3: COLLAPSE

Push the side with the center fold inward (valley-fold) to flatten the pyramid.

STEP 4: GLUE INTO BASE CARD

Fold the base card in half. Apply glue to triangular tab 2 and position the scalloped edge of the glued tab along the fold of the card, centering it vertically (tab 3 should be facing up).

STEP 5: BUILD THE PYRAMID!

Keeping the pyramid collapsed on the left side of the card, apply glue to tab 3 and fold the right side of the card down onto the tent, closing the card. When you open it, the pyramid will pop up. This is a much faster construction than was performed in Egypt!

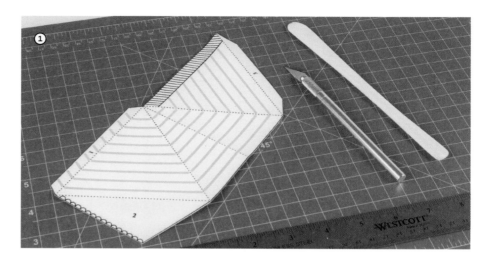

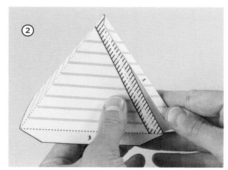

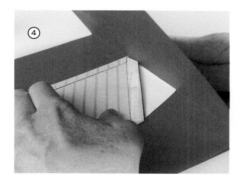

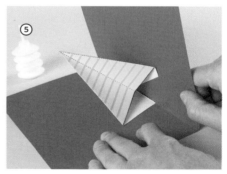

Paper Engineer: Carol Barton
Pop-Up Mechanism: Leaning V-fold pop-up with a floating triangular back
Paper: Pop-up is Passport text 70 lb. smooth; base card is Wausau Astrobrights 65 lb. card stock.
Illustration Style: Digital art

Carousel Pop-Up Book

Who doesn't have fond memories of riding a carousel? Carousel books are like miniature theaters in the round. Emily Martin designed this project, called *Around the House*, to emphasize the circular nature of this type of book structure. You will discover several pop-up techniques as you work your way through the rooms of this house!

INSTRUCTIONS

STEP 1: PREPARE PATTERNS
Download the patterns (or enlarge and photocopy the templates on page 132) and print them onto your papers (see Considerations).

STEP 2: CUT
Cut out all of the house parts with a craft knife and straight-edge; cut out the furnishings using scissors.

STEP 3: RENDER IMAGES
Decorate all of the furnishings for the house using colored pencils. (You can also try crayons, pens, collage, or any other medium you desire.) Be sure to decorate the furnishings on each wall panel and color both sides of the spiraling smoke.

STEP 4: SCORE AND FOLD
Mountain-fold each of the four circular base pieces in half, aligning the sides. Score along all of the dotted and dashed lines: Dashed lines indicate mountain folds and dotted lines indicate valley folds. Note the few solid lines on the interiors of the pieces—these need to be cut as slits and are noted in the assembly instructions for each piece.

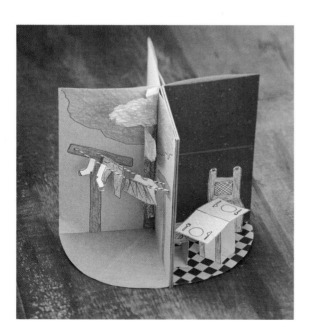

MATERIALS

templates (see page 132)

papers (see considerations)

craft knife

straightedge

scoring tool

cutting mat

scissors

needle, awl, or potter's needle

4 magnets, optional (see Resources, page 143)

PVA glue in a squeeze bottle

heavy thread

colored pencils

binder's board

scrap paper

Japanese hole punch (optional)

CONSIDERATIONS

- When choosing paper for this project, it is best to use papers that are similar in weight for the house walls and furnishings or to use heavier papers for the base and walls and lighter weight papers for the furnishings.

- It is helpful to let the glue dry in between steps, so you may wish to work on several rooms simultaneously. Small weights are also useful when gluing.

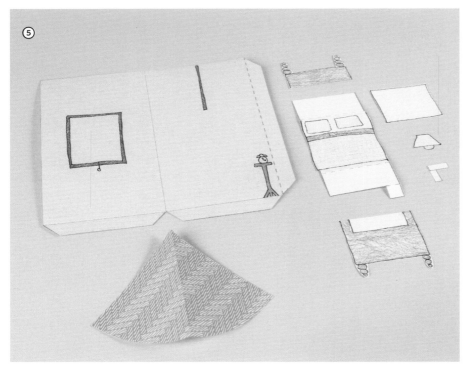

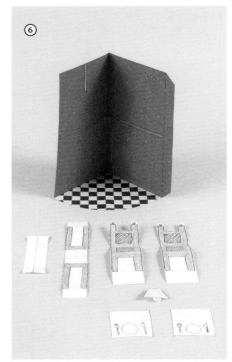

Bedroom parts

Kitchen parts

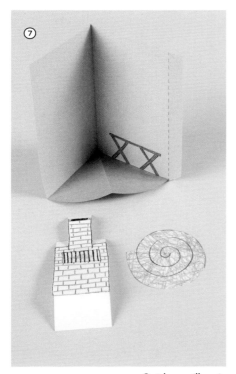

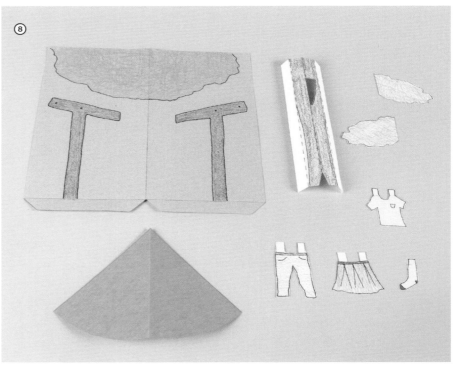

Outdoor grill parts

Outdoor laundry parts

STEP 5: ASSEMBLE THE BEDROOM

A. Glue the wall to the floor: Apply glue to the top of the right-hand side tab of the wall piece and attach the circular floor piece to that tab (do not attach the other side of the floor yet).

Glue footboard: Glue the footboard piece in position on the bed piece.

B. Attach the bed to the wall: Apply glue to the bed tab that folds down under the pillows and glue it in place on the right-hand wall, aligning the bottom of the piece with the right angle of the floor and centering it left to right between the center fold and the nightstand.

C. Attach the bed to the floor: Fold the bed piece up against the wall and put a small glue dot on the small base tab of the bed piece. Fold up the circular floor piece, attaching the floor to the small bed tab. Make sure that the tab attaches only to the right side of the floor's center fold.

Glue the headboard: Apply glue to the back of the headboard and attach it to the wall.

D. Attach the lamp and curtain: Make one large paper spring for the lamp and two small paper springs for the curtain (see "Making a Paper Spring" on page 72). Glue the large spring to the back of the lamp and the two smaller springs to the back top corners of the curtain. Apply glue to the backs of the springs and attach the fixtures in position on the walls.

Finish the floor: Glue the other side of the floor piece to the back wall tab. Fold the page carefully to make sure that everything moves properly.

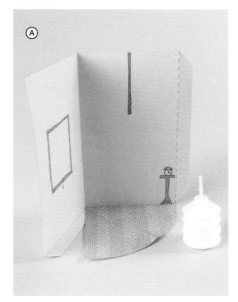

Assembled bedroom

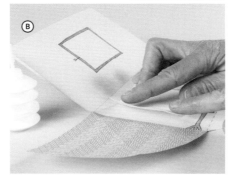

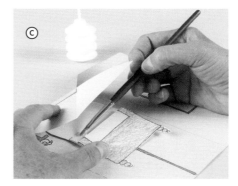

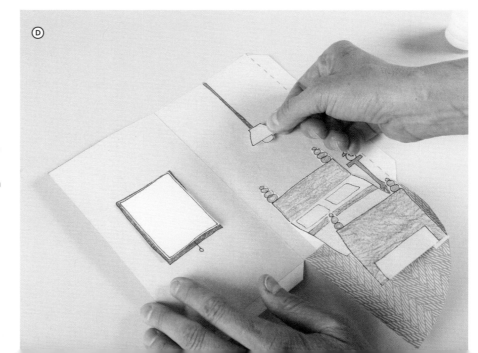

STEP 6: ASSEMBLE THE KITCHEN

Attach the floor: Apply glue to the top of the right-hand side tab of the wall piece and attach the circular floor piece to that tab. Glue the left-hand side of the floor to the wall tab.

A. Affix chairs to walls and floors: Apply glue to the bottom of the base of one chair and glue it to the right-hand side of the floor, off-center and to the right, with the tab tucked up against the wall. Collapse the chair flat onto the floor, and apply glue to the upper back of the chair. Keeping the chair collapsed, fold the floor piece up so that it meets the wall, pressing the glued segment of the chair onto the wall. Attach the second chair to the other wall using the same method, adhering it in the center of the wall.

B. Construct the table: Assemble the small support piece. Cut the two slits as indicated and glue the middle segment of the table support together, leaving the tabs at each end unglued. Glue the tabs on one end of the support to the center of the underside of the table legs. Glue the two parts of the tabletop to the top of the table legs. (The tabletop is cut into two pieces and attached separately; otherwise, there is too much buildup and the table will not open flat.) Glue the base tabs of the table legs to the tabs of the table support. Glue the base tabs of the table legs to the floor, centering them on either side of the fold in the floor.

Attach the lamp to the wall with a spring: Make a small paper spring (see "Making a Paper Spring" on this page) and glue the spring to the back of the lamp piece. Glue the lamp and spring in place on the wall.

Assembled kitchen

MAKING A PAPER SPRING

Springs are mechanisms that make objects, such as lamps or curtains, pop off of the page slightly. To make a spring, overlap two rectangular strips of paper that are the same size and glue them together in the corner so that they are at right angles to each other. Snugly fold the lower paper strip over the top one (which then becomes the lower strip) and continue in this fashion, lower strip over upper strip, until the paper has been folded into a little square spring.

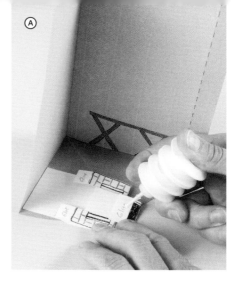

Assembled outdoor grill

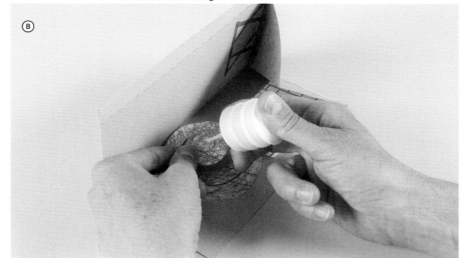

STEP 7: ASSEMBLE THE OUTDOOR GRILL

Attach the floor piece to the wall piece: Glue the folded floor piece to the top of both tabs on the wall piece.

A. Prepare the chimney and attach the grill: Before folding the grill, cut the two slits on the sides of the chimney. Glue the base of the grill onto the left side of the floor panel, near the outer edge of the wall so that the outside corner of the grill is touching the edge of the circular floor panel.

Collapse the grill onto the floor panel and apply glue to the two middle tabs and the upper tab (make sure that you can see the black top of the chimney when it is folded flat). Fold up the wall/floor piece, pressing the glued tabs onto the wall.

B. Stretch the coil of smoke between the chimney and the wall: Put a dab of glue on the outer end of the smoke coil and attach it to the wall at the top of the grill, aligning the flat edge of the coil end with the top of the chimney. Make sure that the entire coil is on the left side of the center fold of the wall and trim the coil if needed.

Put a small glue dot on the inner end of the smoke coil and close the wall/floor piece to attach the smoke coil to the other side of the wall.

STEP 8: ASSEMBLE THE OUTDOOR LAUNDRY

A. Attach the tree to the center fold: Glue one long tab of the tree piece to one side of the wall at the center fold, aligning the top of the tree to the top of the wall. Glue the other long tab to the other side of the wall at the center fold. Glue the two leaf pieces to either side of the tree piece near the top, making sure that the leaf pieces do not

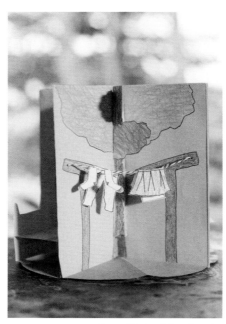
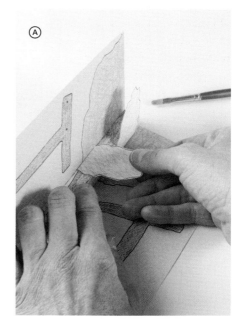

Assembled outdoor laundry

stick out of the book and do not run into each other when closed.

Attach the floor: Glue the folded floor piece to the top of both tabs on the wall piece.

B. Sew the threads: Poke four holes through the wall marked on the clothesline. Thread a large needle with heavy thread and starting from the back of the left-hand wall, sew through the hole closest to the fold of the wall. Glue the end of the thread to the back of the wall to hold it in place. Bring the thread across to the other wall, threading it through the hole closest to the fold. Bring the thread back into the page by sewing through the wall and then thread it through the last hole, taking it to the back side again.

Adjust the tension in the thread to allow the wall/floor piece to open fully without the threads sagging. Trim the thread and glue the end to the back of the wall. The span of thread on the other wall can also be glued down.

C. Glue the various laundry pieces over the threads using the individual tabs.

STEP 9: ASSEMBLE THE BOOK

A. Connect the rooms: Connect the rooms to each other by applying glue to the tabs on the right side of the first three rooms. The Outdoor Laundry Room has no tab and will be the last room added to the book.

B. Make book covers: Cut two pieces of binder's board to 7" × 3¾" (17.8 × 9.5 cm), the same size that the walls are when folded shut. Cut two pieces of paper to 8" × 4¾" (20.3 × 12 cm) to cover the boards. Apply glue to one of the pieces of binder's board and affix

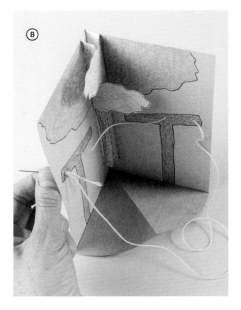

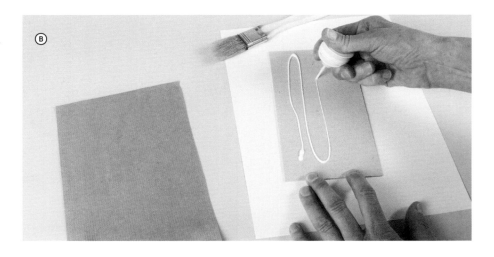

it to the back side of one of the cover papers, centering it on the paper. Trim the corners of the cover papers (this is called *mitering the corners*).

Carefully glue one edge at a time and fold the cover paper over onto the binder's board. Repeat with the other board to make the second cover.

C. Measure and cut two sheets of rectangular paper to fill in the spaces on the back side of each covered board to reduce warping of the glued boards.

Attach the covers: Attach the boards to the front and back of the two outer rooms by applying a small bead of glue around the edges of the boards. Alternatively, you can use double-sided tape. Attach a title panel if you desire.

Displaying the Carousel: Books are meant to be read, but artists' books can also be shown. This book can be displayed as an accordion or in the round, and it is handy to build in a mechanism for holding the covers together if it is to be displayed in the round. Two ideas for making this possible are to embed tiny magnets in the binder's board prior to covering the boards with paper or attach to ribbons between the end walls and the covers.

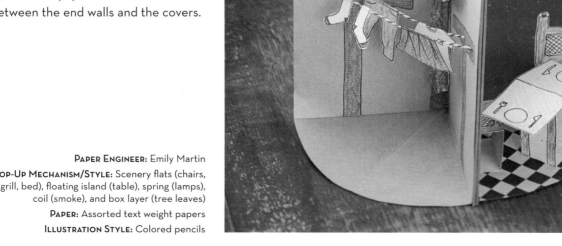

PAPER ENGINEER: Emily Martin
POP-UP MECHANISM/STYLE: Scenery flats (chairs, grill, bed), floating island (table), spring (lamps), coil (smoke), and box layer (tree leaves)
PAPER: Assorted text weight papers
ILLUSTRATION STYLE: Colored pencils

Tunnel Book

The pages of this unique book form are stretched open rather than turned, and the window-page format allows the entire book to be viewed at once, like a mini theater. Paper engineer Ed Hutchins has studied and adapted this structure for the past twenty years and shares his wisdom in this tunnel book, filled with canaries, bluebirds, and a cardinal. Feel free to add your own touches—a nest with baby birds, a visiting owl, a squirrel, clouds, leaves, blossoms, a blue sky in the background, or a moon on the black board. The sky is the limit!

A Brief History of Tunnel Books

Tunnel books owe their history to the long line of optical experiments that led to the development of the motion picture. In 1437, Leone Battista produced a small box with a peephole that revealed scenes that could be viewed in perspective. In the 1600s, traveling showmen carried peep-show boxes on their backs, featuring interchangeable pages with cutout cardboard panels depicting religious, historical, and mythical scenes. The advent of printing allowed for the production of smaller peepshows and eventually, concertina hinges were used to attach panels, creating the present-day tunnel book. In fact, there was a trend to celebrate major events with the production of a commemorative peepshow: the opening of the Thames River Tunnel in 1843 (where the tunnel book most likely got its name), the New York World's Fair in 1939, and Queen Elizabeth's Silver Jubilee in 1977, among others.

Paper Tip

The secret to making dynamic tunnel books is to use stiff covers that won't buckle when the book is opened and closed, firm paper for the center panels, and a flexible paper for the side hinges so that the book closes flat.

MATERIALS

bird and branch templates
  (see page 140)
2 pieces of 4" × 6" (10.2 × 15.2 cm)
  mat board
2 pieces of 4" × 6" (10.2 × 15.2 cm)
  card stock
6 pieces of 3½" × 3" (9 × 7.6 cm)
  strong, flexible paper with the
  grain running in the 3" (7.6 cm)
  direction
pen
straightedge
pencil cutting mat
craft knife
white glue
glue brush

INSTRUCTIONS

STEP 1: CREATE THE VIEWING FRAME
Take one of the pieces of mat board and draw a border on the back measuring ¾" (2 cm) on the top and sides and 1" (2.5 cm) on the bottom. Cut along these lines to create a frame and mark "top" on the back of the frame.

STEP 2: CUT THE WINDOWS
Using the mat board frame that you just cut as a template, trace the window shape onto the two pieces of 4" × 6" (10.2 × 15.2 cm) card stock and then cut out the two windows. Mark "top" on the back of each one.

STEP 3: CUT BIRDS AND BRANCHES
Download the bird and branch patterns (or enlarge and photocopy the templates on page 140) and print them onto the back side of appropriately colored card stocks. Fold the paper in half to save on work time and cut two birds at a time. Cut small triangles from scrap paper for the beaks and glue the beaks and wings onto the birds. Add eyes and other embellishments to the birds and branches.

STEP 4: LAY OUT THE PAGES
Lay out the pages of the book: the back cover (solid mat board), the front cover (mat board frame), and the two inside paper frames. Position the birds and branches on the frames to create the scene as shown, or play around with your own positioning. Glue the bird and branch pieces onto the front cover, inside frames, and back cover.

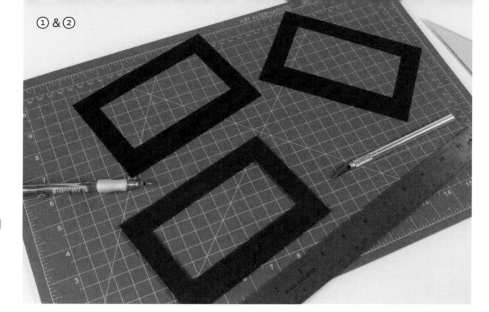

STEP 5: MAKE THE SIDE HINGES

Fold one of the side hinge papers in half, short side to short side. Unfold, turn it over, and fold each edge in to the center to create an accordion fold that looks like an *M*. Place an X on one of the end panels. Repeat with the remaining five hinge pieces.

STEP 6: ASSEMBLE THE BOOK

Assemble the book from front to back:

A. Place the front cover facedown on your work surface. Take one hinge piece and glue the panel marked × to the edge of the cover, orienting it so that the first fold on the accordion-folded hinge lines up with the outside edge of the cover. Repeat this process on the opposite side of the cover, attaching a second hinge.

B. Hold the first inner frame facedown (making sure the top is oriented properly) and slip it in between the last two folds on both sides of the hinge. Carefully apply glue to the back side of the last hinge panel and glue the hinge onto the back of the frame on both sides: Don't be too concerned if the exposed panels fail to line up exactly with the edges of the frame—push the edges of the frame snuggly into the folds of the side hinges on both sides and glue the frame in place. When complete, the hinges will fall into place nicely.

Repeat steps A and B to attach the next inner frame and then the back cover, making sure that each piece is properly oriented before gluing in place.

Optional: Add a text sheet to the back of the book and/or a title label on the front cover. You can also incorporate text into the pages of the book.

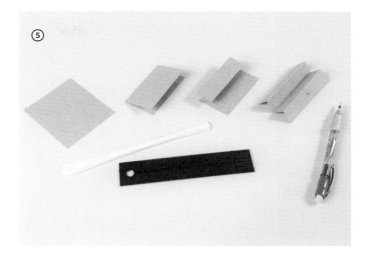

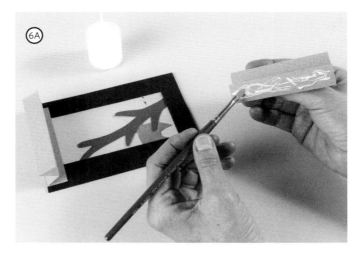

Paper Engineer: Ed Hutchins
Pop-Up Mechanism/Style: Tunnel book
Papers: Crescent mounting board (front and back covers), Canson Mi-Teintes paper (birds and branches), Canson Ingres paper (side hinges)
Illustration Style: Collage

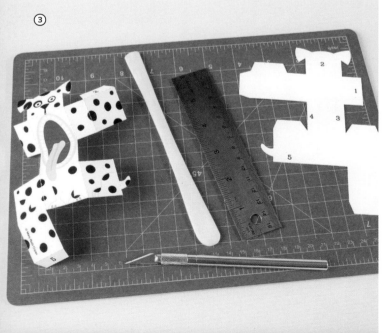

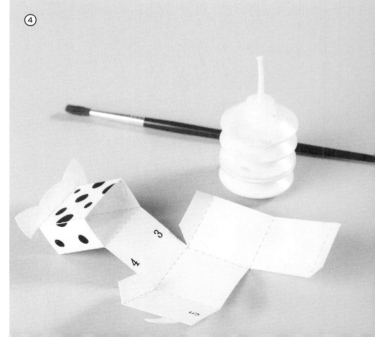

Puppy Puppet

This adorable movable finger puppet was developed by paper engineer Mary Beth Cryan as a promotional piece for her illustration and paper engineering business back in 2009. Its shape makes it easily adaptable for a variety of characters: Print out the blank template and illustrate your favorite human, animal, or imaginary creature!

INSTRUCTIONS

STEP 1: PREP AND CUT

Download the pattern (or enlarge and photocopy the templates on page 136) and print it onto card stock. Make sure the numbers appear on the tabs on the front side and on the areas on the back. You can write the numbers onto the template if they weren't printed because they won't be visible on the final puppy.

STEP 2: ILLUSTRATE

Use markers, colored pencils, or crayons to illustrate the front of the finger puppet. Use the template as a guide for illustrating the various body parts.

STEP 3: CUT AND SCORE

Cut the puppet out along the solid black lines. Score along all of the lines that indicate folds. Mountain-fold each scored line except for the fold in the center of the puppy's mouth, which is a valley fold.

STEP 4: GLUE

Glue tab 1 on the front to area 1 on the back, aligning the folded edges and creating the rectangular space. Finish forming the puppy's head by gluing tab 2 on the front to area 2 on the back.

Glue tabs 3 and 4 on the front to areas 3 and 4 on the back. Finish forming the puppy's body by gluing tab 5 on the front to area 5 on the back.

STEP 5: ACTION!

Slide your fingers into the back of the finger puppet and move them to make the mouth open and close.

PAPER ENGINEER: Mary Beth Cryan
POP-UP MECHANISM/STYLE: boxes with a hinge
PAPER: Card stock
ILLUSTRATION STYLE: Digital art

MATERIALS

puppy templates (see page 136)
card stock
markers, crayons, or colored
   pencils
glue
glue brush
bone folder

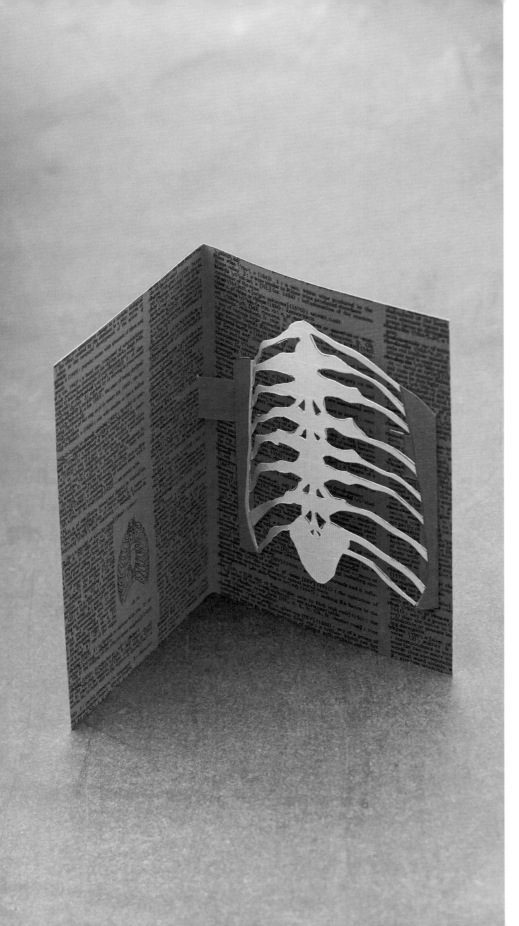

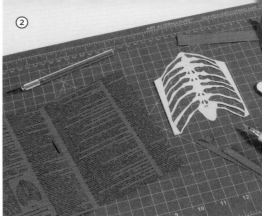

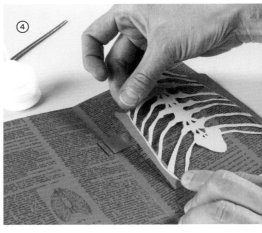

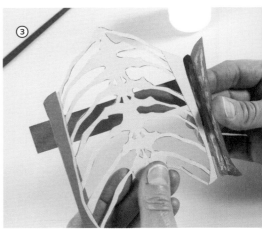

PAPER ENGINEER: Yoojin Kim
POP-UP MECHANISM/STYLE: Pull tab
PAPER: Colored card stocks
ILLUSTRATION STYLE: Photocopy

Pull-Tab Rib Cage

Artist Yoojin Kim translates forms found in human anatomy into pop-ups. She is captivated by the overlapping qualities that exist between the function of pop-ups and how a human body works. Pivots and levers resemble the movements of human tendons and joints and the way that muscles move. This project features an adaptation of the pull-tab cylinder technique. As the spread is opened, a strap pulls the tab to raise the rib cage from the flat surface.

Rib Cage Trivia

Here's an interesting fact about the human rib cage: When the Flemish anatomist Vesalius noted in 1543 that humans have twenty-four ribs (twelve on each side), he set off a wave of controversy. It had been assumed from the Biblical story of Adam and Eve that men's ribs would number one less than women's. Variations in the number of ribs do occur, and about one in two hundred to five hundred people have an additional cervical rib; these extra rib-holders are predominantly female.

INSTRUCTIONS

STEP 1: PREPARE BACKGROUND AND PRINT

I photocopied a dictionary page onto card stock to create a background for my rib cage. You can use a plain card stock, purchase a printed card stock, illustrate the background, or make a collage to accent the ribs. Once you've got your papers, download the patterns for the base card and rib cage (or enlarge and photocopy the templates on page 138) and print them onto your prepared card stock.

STEP 2: CUT AND SCORE

Cut out the card base, the two rib cage side pieces, and the rib cage using a craft knife. Cut the three slits in the card base. Score along the central dotted line on the card base and valley-fold it in half. Score along the dashed lines on the two rib cage side pieces and mountain-fold each one along those lines.

STEP 3: GLUE THE SIDE PIECES

Glue the inside of both folded rib cage side pieces, gluing both sides of the fold and sandwiching the matching sides of the rib cage into the glued areas.

STEP 4: THREAD STRAP AND MOUNT RIB CAGE

Thread the strap through the right-hand slit in the card base from front to back and then thread it back into the card through the slit along the dotted line. Carefully lift the left side of the rib cage and apply glue to the back side of the rib cage side piece. Attach it to the base along the dotted line, taking care not to get glue on the strap.

STEP 5: ASSEMBLE

Tuck the loose end of the strap into the slit on the left side of the base while folding the base page in half. Close the card completely, fold the end of the strap over, and glue it to the card base. Let the glue dry briefly. Open the card and watch your rib cage slide into three dimensions!

MATERIALS

templates (see page 138)
card stock
craft knife
scissors
glue
scoring tool
straightedge
cutting mat

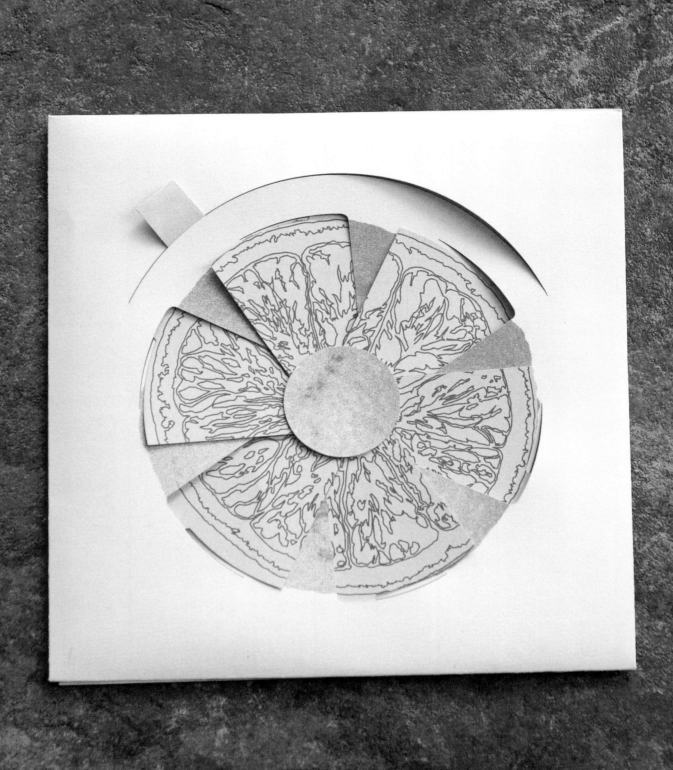

Volvelle with Six Slots

A volvelle *is a rotating paper mechanism.* Early volvelles, often used to make astronomical calculations, were constructed out of disks of paper that were held onto the page of a book with a length of linen thread. Book artist Julie Chen adapted the design of this mechanism from a form she saw in Ernest Nister's *Land of Sweet Surprises, A Revolving Picture Book,* first published in 1897. This volvelle variation offers the potential for creating an illusion of one image "dissolving" into another as the tab is swung from one end of the curved slot to the other end.

INSTRUCTIONS

STEP 1: PREP, CUT, AND SCORE

Download the patterns (or enlarge and photocopy the templates on page 141) and print them onto the back side of two sheets of card stock. Cut out the wheel, the square piece, and the small circle using a craft knife and illustrate as desired. Use a sharp blade to ensure clean cuts—this will make the six-slot volvelle fairly easy to assemble. Trim, or miter, the corners on the square piece as indicated, cut on all of the solid interior lines, and score along the lines indicating folds. Cut the third piece of card stock into a 7" (17.8 cm) square. (This will be used to cover the back of the volvelle, hiding the mechanism.)

MATERIALS

templates (see page 141)

3 sheets of 8½" × 11"
 (21.6 × 28 cm) card stock

craft knife

circle cutter (optional)

glue stick

ruler

white glue

glue brush

pencil

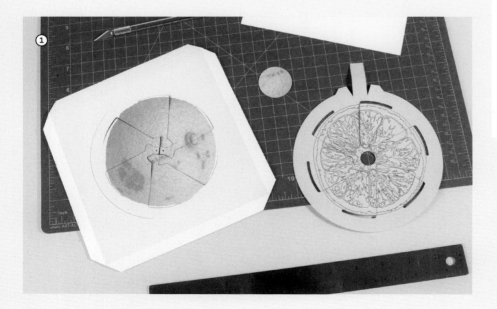

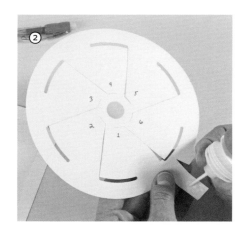

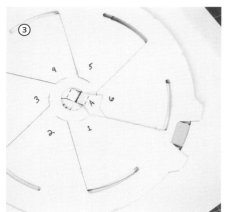

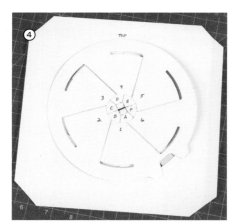

STEP 2: MARK AND FOLD TABS

Fold the tab on the wheel piece in half along the score line and glue it to itself using white glue. Draw two small dots on the ends of tabs A and D (in the little boxes beyond the score lines, as indicated) on the front side of the piece.

STEP 3: THREAD FIRST TAB

Hold the square piece upside down with the letters oriented so that you can read them and place the wheel (upside down) on top with the numbers oriented so that you can read them, too. Carefully thread tab A (from underneath) through the slot at the top of panel 1. After tab A is in the slot, carefully thread the pull tab through the curved slot at the bottom of the square piece so that it is now on the front side of the mechanism. Make sure the two tabs on either side of the pull tab are not threaded with the pull tab and keep the pull tab in this position as you thread the remaining tabs through the corresponding slots in the wheel.

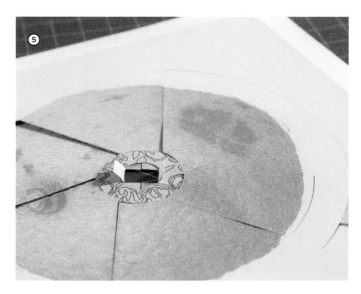

STEP 4: THREAD REMAINING TABS INTO PANEL SLOTS

Carefully thread tab B (from underneath) through the slot at the top of panel 2. Continue threading tabs C through F into the slots on panels 3 through 6 in this manner. Once all the tabs are slotted through, you should be able to see all the letters on the tabs (A through F).

STEP 5: FOLD CENTER TABS

Fold the two tabs marked with the dots toward the front along the score lines.

STEP 6: ATTACH THE BACK PANEL

Start by gluing the back panel to the folder on one of the folded margins (a glue stick works well for this). Next, put a small dot of white glue on each lettered tab and stick the back panel onto the back of the mechanism, applying pressure (with your hand or a scoring tool) over the areas where you placed the dots of glue in the center. Do not glue the other three folded margins yet.

STEP 7: ATTACH THE SMALL CIRCLE

Turn the whole mechanism over and place a small dot of white glue on top of the dots printed on the two central tabs that you folded over to the front. Attach the central circle element to the tabs and press firmly.

STEP 8: TEST YOUR MECHANISM

Slide the tab slowly to the right (A through D). The scene on the wheel should start to appear through the six angled slots. If the mechanism does not slide smoothly, check to see whether there are rough edges along any of the cuts that need trimming. All cuts must be very smooth for the mechanism to operate properly. Once it turns smoothly, fold in the remaining three margins along the edges of the folder and adhere them to the inside of the back panel with a glue stick.

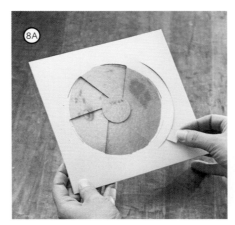

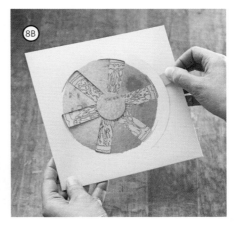

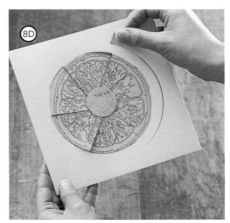

PAPER ENGINEER: Julie Chen
POP-UP MECHANISM/STYLE: Volvelle (rotating disk)
PAPER: Springhill Digital Index 110 lb. by International Paper
ILLUSTRATION STYLE: Digital art by Julie Chen and Jill Lerner

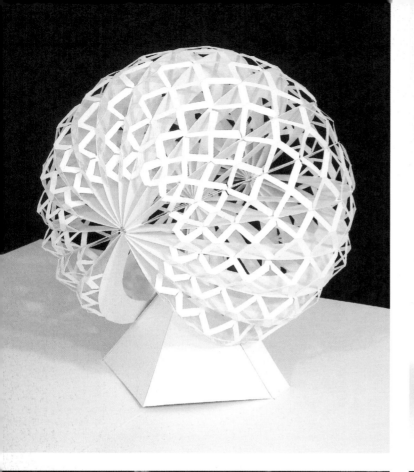

CHAPTER 3

Gallery: Discovering New Realms by Turning the Page

Artists have been engineering with paper for centuries and today their innovations are being used in artwork, trade publications, advertising, and more. As you flip through these pages, I think you will gain an appreciation for the versatility of the medium and the ingenuity of these artists. All of them are contemporary artists working in the field, and many of them have an online presence. I encourage you to explore their work online (some of them even have free project templates on their websites). Many of these paper engineers also have published pop-up books on the market. Check your bookstore or library and experience their work first-hand as you turn the pages.

PROJECTS AT LEFT (TOP TO BOTTOM; LEFT TO RIGHT):
Untitled, PETER DAHMEN;
Old Mother Hubbard in
San Francisco, PAUL JOHNSON;
Alcazar Big Pop, DAVID CARTER;
Pigeon, SHAWN SHEEHY

Shelby Arnold

Shelby Arnold is a professional paper engineer who makes pop-up books, artist's books, and origami. She works for artist Robert Sabuda, creating children's pop-up books and pop-up cards for the Museum of Modern Art. She has a degree in graphic design from Pratt Institute and spends her free time playing with paper electronics at her local hackerspace, NYC Resistor, in Brooklyn.

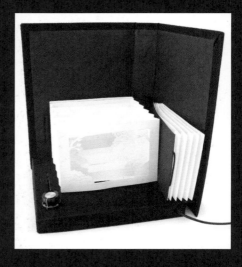

TITLE: *Tunnel Book*
DESCRIPTION: Laser-cut paper, Arduino micro-controller, LEDs. A stage containing electronics folds down to create a platform, and above the stage three separate laser-cut, accordion-folded scenes can be pulled out.

Photos: Shelby Arnold

Andrew Baron

Andrew Baron began creating pop-ups in 1995 at White Heat LTD in Santa Fe, New Mexico, following twenty-one years of restoring mechanical antiques. He has been fortunate to work on an unusually wide variety of pop-up forms with some of the world's greatest illustrators. Baron's paper engineering is notable for its integration of innovative mechanical and kinetic elements within the dimensional structure. In an unusual turn of events, Baron's pop-up work led him back into the world of machines when he was asked by Philadelphia's Franklin Institute to restore their ca. 1800 Maillardet automaton. The automaton was a key inspiration for Brian Selznick's book *The Invention of Hugo Cabret* and the Academy Award–winning film *Hugo*. It was Selznick's friend and Baron's pop-up collaborator Paul Zelinsky who first suggested that Baron could do in real life what Hugo does in the story. Baron's books have received numerous national and international awards, including the Movable Book Society's Meggendorfer Prize.

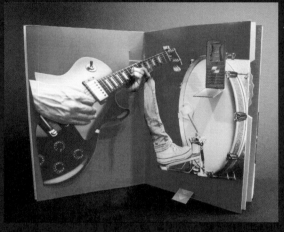

TITLE: *Johanna* (from *Sony Ericsson Pop-Up Book*), 2007
DESCRIPTION: Trade show promotion with live models. The titles were based on the model of the phone featured in each spread, 14" × 10¼" (35.6 × 26 cm), open.

TITLE: *Smaug* (from *The Hobbit: A 3-D Pop-Up Adventure*), 1999
DESCRIPTION: Illustrations by John Howe, conceptual artist for *The Lord of the Rings* trilogy, 15½" × 10½" (39.4 × 26.7 cm), open.

TITLE: *Percy's Playground* (from *Four Feathers in Percy's Park*), 1998
DESCRIPTION: Illustrations by Nick Butterworth, 38½" × 9½" × 9½" (97.8 × 24 × 24 cm) (panorama with all four scenes open). Individual environments are 9½" (24 cm) cube.

Photos: Andrew Baron

Carol Barton

Carol Barton's design of books and sculptural pop-up forms grows out of a love of creative play. Barton is a book artist, curator, and teacher who has published her own artist's editions as well as three award-winning books on how to make pop-ups, *The Pocket Paper Engineer: How to Make Pop-Ups Step-by-Step*, Volumes 1, 2, and 3. She has organized local and national shows and her work is exhibited internationally. She is on the faculty at The University of the Arts in Philadelphia and the Corcoran College of Art and Design in Washington, D.C.

TITLE: *Home Dreams* (page 1), 1997
DESCRIPTION: Acrylic, laser printing, pop-ups,
6" × 4" × 44" (15.2 × 10.2 × 111.8 cm).

TITLE: *Five Luminous Towers, A Book to be Read in the Dark*, 2001
DESCRIPTION: Offset lithography, batteries, light, fiber-optic filament,
11½" × 7½" × 3" (29.2 × 20 × 7.6 cm).

Photos: Carol Barton

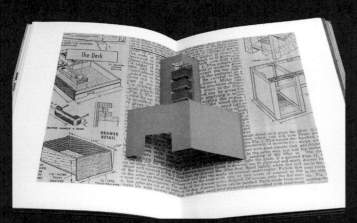

TITLE: *Instructions for Assembly*, 2003
DESCRIPTION: Ink-jet printing, 7" × 2⅝" × 70" (17.8 × 6.7 × 177.8 cm).

Marion Bataille

Marion Bataille is a French graphic designer working in Paris. She is the author of several books for children in which she plays with the shape of letters. In 2006, Bataille produced thirty handmade copies of *OP-UP*, which she presented as an artist's book in a Paris gallery. The book was discovered by the French publisher Albin Michel. *OP-UP* was published with the title *ABC3D* in 2009 by Albin Michel and twelve copublishers worldwide. Her second book, published by Chronicle Books, is called *Numero* and features the numbers one through ten.

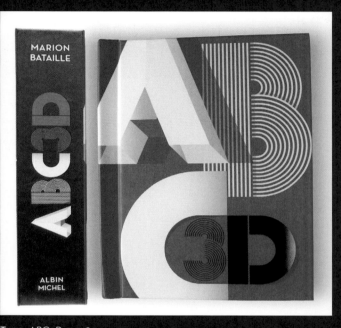

TITLE: *M (from ABC3D)*, 2008
DESCRIPTION: *M* is for *maison* ("house" in French), 5½" × 7" (14 × 18 cm)
Photo: Marion Bataille

TITLE: *ABC3D*, 2008
DESCRIPTION: Book cover, 5½" × 7" (14 × 18 cm)
Photo: Marion Bataille/Albin Michel

TITLE: *IJ (from ABC3D)*, 2008
DESCRIPTION: *I* and *J* share a dot. *Avoir un point commun* is a French expression that means "to have something in common," 5½" × 7" (14 × 18 cm)
Photo: Marion Bataille

Monika Brandrup

Monika Brandrup is the vice president and creative director of Up With Paper, LLC, a leading international pop-up greeting card and stationery company, as well as Jumping Jack Press, which is the publishing division for innovative pop-up books for both children and adults.

Up With Paper's greeting cards are available for all seasons and occasions. Brandrup works with as many as fifty illustrators and fifteen paper engineers globally (some of whom are well known and others who are just entering the industry) to come up with designs for the markets it serves.

Over the years, Up With Paper has been recognized for developing some of the most outstanding greeting cards in the industry, winning more than sixty-five LOUIE Awards as well as the industry's highest honor, Card of the Year, in 2004, for one of Brandrup's original card designs.

TITLE: *Snow Queen*, 2013
DESCRIPTION: Illustrator and engineer: Yevgeniya Yeretskaya. This unique retelling of the classic Hans Christian Andersen fairy tale includes seven dazzling spreads that come to life with a stunning combination of classic illustration and innovative paper engineering.

Photos: Aaron Borchetta

The celebration gets started

With a cannon ball splish!

JB PARTY

slide

slide

TITLE: *Splish Splash Dog Bash*, 2007
DESCRIPTION: Engineer: Bruce Foster; illustrator: Jason O'Malley. Jumping Jack Press pop-up book, featuring eight delightful spreads of pop-up fun. When the owners are away, the dogs will play—in the pool! Join a neighborhood of mischievous dogs at their annual pool party.

BABY

TITLE: *Crib Animals*, 2009
DESCRIPTION: Artist: Colleen O'Hara; engineer: Renee Jablow; 10 pt C1S with glitter and spot UV, 5¼" × 10½" (13.3 × 26.7 cm) open at 90 degrees.

David Carter

David Carter began his art career at Intervisual Communications, a company specializing in pop-ups in advertising. Carter, who had never seen a pop-up book, soon became the art director there. During his tenure, he met some of the early paper engineers—John Strejan, Jim Diaz, Tor Lokvig, Jan Pienkowski, David Pelham—and had the opportunity to work with them on the design, illustration, and publishing aspects of their books.

Carter eventually had the opportunity to produce his own books at Intervisual, and his pop-up book, *How Many Bugs in a Box?*, published by Simon & Schuster in 1988, was a huge success (more than one million copies sold in the United States). At the time, there were no books like this in the American market.

After his formative years at Intervisual Communications, Carter struck out on his own, and today he is the author of more than seventy pop-up books, including his well-known *One Red Dot* series. He has been an innovator in other realms, producing a limited edition of twenty-five thousand pop-up albums for the band Coldplay, among other projects. Many of Carter's books are geared toward children, and he has always spent time in schools.

With fellow paper engineer Jim Diaz, he put together *The Elements of Pop-Up*, a thorough guide to creating pop-ups, which includes a glossary and real pop-ups as illustrations, allowing readers to see and interact with the mechanics of basic pop-up structures.

TITLE: *Alcazar Big Pop*, 2009, 2012
DESCRIPTION: At 8' × 4' (2.4 × 1.2 m) (when open) this pop-up is Carter's largest piece. He originally created it for an exhibition at the Blue Line Gallery in Roseville, California, and this one was made for the library Alcazar in Marseille, France.

Photos (above & right) David Carter

Title: *Hide and Seek, 2012*
Description: Art pop-up book featuring hidden objects, 9" × 9" (23 × 23 cm).

Photos (top, left & right) Courtesy of Albin Michel

Title: *Hide and Seek, 2012*
Description: Art pop-up book featuring hidden objects, 9" × 9" (23 × 23 cm).

Photo: Courtesy of Albin Michel

Title: *One Red Dot, 2005*
Description: Pop-up page spread, 9" × 9" (23 × 23 cm).

Julie Chen

While in the master of arts program at Mills College in Oakland, California, in book arts, Julie Chen founded Flying Fish Press and started producing limited-edition artist's books, incorporating letterpress printing, movable parts, and pop-ups. At the time, she looked to the model of the fine-press book production, which is focused on fine printing and typography. But Chen was attracted to the structure of the book. Her style soon began to emerge, and she frequently found herself asking "What is a book?" and "Is this a book?" Chen's definition of a book is broad, but at the core she finds the act of reading and the element of time to be the essential parts that constitute a book.

Her knowledge comes from dissecting and looking at old pop-up books or reverse engineering to see how these old books were constructed. Chen doesn't use math or geometry to design her pop-ups, but instead she builds models by cutting paper, taping it together, and sometimes simply smashing or collapsing a fold to see how to engineer her ideas.

Chen's books all have a conceptual component, and this allows her work to span a wide range of topics. Her book, *Panorama*, deals with climate change. Chen explains that after conducting research on the topic, she realized the book needed movement in order to portray the gravity of the situation. When the reader turns the page, the book confronts them—literally—as huge pop-ups (the page spread is 40-inches [101.6 cm] wide) protrude into the viewer's personal space. The book is also interactive, requiring the reader to lift flaps and unfold pages to find the text and discover the content. At the same time as the viewer is confronted, he or she is also rewarded with beautiful pop-up landscapes. This book reminds us to appreciate the beauty of our surroundings and what we have, while calling us to action by prompting us to alter our behavior so that this beauty will be preserved.

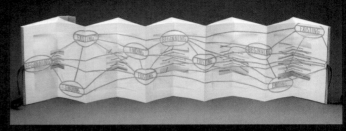

TITLE: *Cat's Cradle, 2013*
DESCRIPTION: Text and image by Julie Chen, published by Flying Fish Press, Berkeley, California.
Photos: Sibila Savage

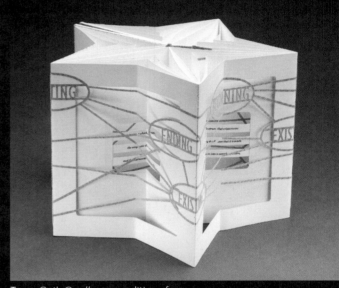

TITLE: *Cat's Cradle*, 2013, edition of 50
DESCRIPTION: Text and image by Julie Chen, published by Flying Fish Press, Berkeley, California. Book size (closed): 5³⁄₈" × 8¹⁄₁₆" × 1" (13.7 × 20.5 × 2.5 cm). Book width (open): 30" (76.2 cm).

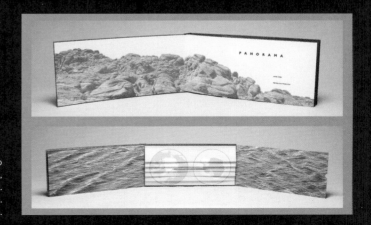

TITLE: *Panorama*, 2008, edition of 100
DESCRIPTION: Text and image by Julie Chen, published by Flying Fish Press, Berkeley, California. Box size: 10¼" × 20⅝" × 2" (26 × 51 × 5 cm). Book size (closed): 9½" × 20¼" × 1¼" (24 × 51.4 × 3.2 cm). Book width (open): 60" (152.4 cm).

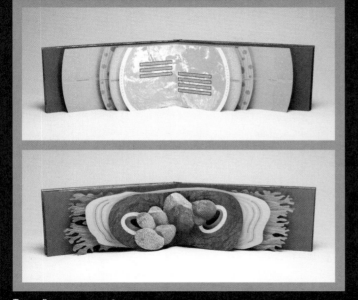

Title: *Panorama*, 2008
Description: Text and image by Julie Chen, published by Flying Fish Press, Berkeley, California.

Title: *Invented Landscape*, 2010, edition of 50
Description: Text and image by Julie Chen, published by Flying Fish Press, Berkeley, California. Box size: 5½" × 9¾" × 2¾" (14 × 24.8 × 7 cm). Book size (closed): 5" × 9¾" × 1¾" (12.7 × 24.8 × 4.4 cm). Book width (open): 66" (167.6 cm).

Title: *Invented Landscape*, 2010
Description: Text and image by Julie Chen, published by Flying Fish Press, Berkeley, California.

Elod Beregszaszi

Elod Beregszaszi calls the way that he manipulates paper "paper space exploration." He founded Popupology Studio in 2006 to develop and find applications for the genre of cutting and folding form from a single sheet of paper known as origamic architecture. He shares his discoveries and provides a learning resource by sharing templates for many paper-folding projects online (see Resources, page 143).

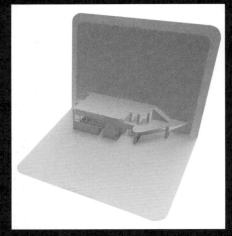

TITLE: *Corbusier Villa*, 2012
DESCRIPTION: Cut and folded from a single sheet of white superfine cartridge paper (220 gsm) with a colored Chromatico transparency paper backing, 5¾" × 4" (144 × 103 mm) when closed.

Photos: Elod Beregszaszi

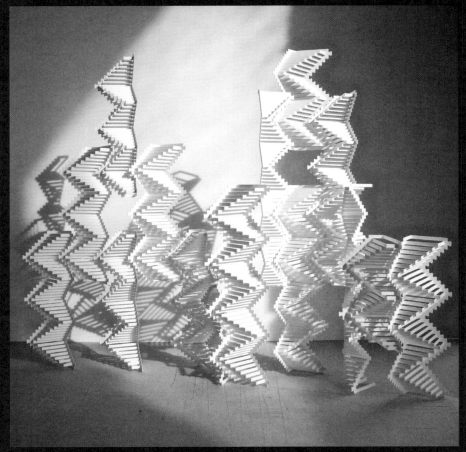

TITLE: *Tender Pixel*, 2011
DESCRIPTION: Cut and folded from white superfine cartridge paper (220 gsm), dimensions variable (modular construction).

TITLE: *Love Birds*, 2011
DESCRIPTION: Cut and folded from a single sheet of white superfine cartridge paper (220 gsm), 3½" × 2¼" (86 × 56 mm) when closed.

Mary Beth Cryan

Mary Beth Cryan illustrates and engineers all of her projects and then licenses her creations in the form of greeting cards, books, craft kits, magazines, stationery, children's toys, and party products. Cryan has a dozen paper craft books in print, and she has worked with companies such as the Museum of Modern Art New York, American Girl, Peter Pauper Press, Dover Publications, *Highlights*, and *Ladybug* magazine. Vector art is her medium of choice and "that's clever" is her favorite compliment.

TITLE: *Stegosaurus* (from the book *Paper Craft Dinosaurs*, 2012)
DESCRIPTION: Written, illustrated, and engineered by Mary Beth Cryan, published by Peter Pauper Press, vector art and card stock. Assembled: 8" × 2½" × 3½" (20.3 × 6.4 × 9 cm). Unassembled: 8" × 11" (20.3 × 28 cm).
Photo: Eric Widor

TITLE: *Paper Bobble Head* (from the kit *Paper Bobble Heads: Monsters*, 2011)
DESCRIPTION: Illustrated and engineered by Mary Beth Cryan, published by NPW, vector art and card stock. Assembled: 3½" × 2" × 2" (9 × 5.1 × 5.1 cm). Unassembled: 6" × 6" (15.2 × 15.2 cm).
Photo: John Selby

TITLE: *Portable Yule Log Greeting Card*, 2010
DESCRIPTION: Illustrated and engineered by Mary Beth Cryan, published by The Museum of Modern Art New York, vector art and card stock. Closed: 5" × 7" (12.7 × 17.8 cm). Opened: 6" × 5" × 5" (15.2 × 12.7 × 12.7 cm).
Photo: Mary Beth Cryan

Peter Dahmen

German artist Peter Dahmen's claim to fame came when a short film of one of his paper sculptures appeared on YouTube in 2010. To date it has been seen by millions of viewers, and Dahmen has received commissions from companies worldwide. In addition to collaborating with card manufacturing companies, he has designed pop-up sculptures for the American magician Marco Tempest and has constructed a giant pop-up card (approx. 10.5 × 5.2 m tall) for a press conference at the 2011 International Motor Show in Frankfurt/Main, Germany. Dahmen also creates artistic pop-up sculptures in his studio.

TITLE: *Untitled*, 1989
DESCRIPTION: Paper and card stock, approx. 25½" × 19¾"× 11½" (650 × 500 × 290 mm) (open), approx. 13" × 9¾"× ¼" (325 × 500 × 8 mm) (closed).

TITLE: *Peacock*, 2010
DESCRIPTION: Printed paper, card stock, approx. 420 × 210 × 120 mm (open), approx. 148.5 × 210 × 21 mm (closed).

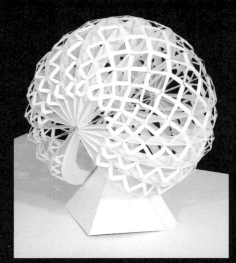

TITLE: *Untitled*, 1990
DESCRIPTION: Paper and card stock, approx. 25½" × 19¾"× 7½" (650 × 500 × 190 mm)

Bruce Foster

With more than forty pop-up books on his résumé, Bruce Foster doesn't confine himself to any one genre or target age. He has designed books for children and families (*America's National Parks*, which won a Gold IPPY in 2013); for adults, movies, and educational purposes (such as a pop-up human brain for MacMillan Publishing); and for museums. He strives to find the magic in each interpretation; to create an interplay of motion and form in achieving the realization of the pop-up. Foster lives in Houston with his wife, Lori.

TITLE: *Taj Mahal* (from *Architectural Wonders: A Pop-Up Gallery of the World's Most Amazing Marvels*), 2008
DESCRIPTION: Published by Thunder Bay Press, produced by becker&mayer!, 10" × 12" × 1½" (25.4 × 30.5 × 3.8 cm), paper engineering by Bruce Foster, illustrations by Dan Brown.

Photo: Bruce Foster

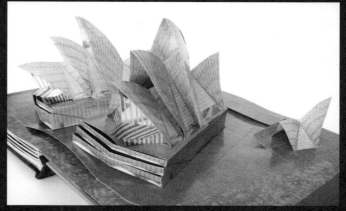

TITLE: *Sydney Opera House* (from *Architectural Wonders: A Pop-Up Gallery of the World's Most Amazing Marvels*), 2008
DESCRIPTION: Published by Thunder Bay Press, produced by becker&mayer!, 10" × 12" × 1½" (25.4 × 30.5 × 3.8 cm), paper engineering by Bruce Foster, illustrations by Dan Brown.

Photo: Bruce Foster

TITLE: *Hogwarts School of Witchcraft and Wizardry* (from *Harry Potter: A Pop-Up Book*, 2010)
DESCRIPTION: Published by Insight Editions, 9" × 11¼" × 1¾" (23 × 28.6 × 4.4 cm), paper engineering by Bruce Foster, illustrations by Andrew Williamson.

Photo: Courtesy of Insight Editions

Colette Fu

Colette Fu is an interdisciplinary artist who uses her vivid photographs in various forms of collage and collapsible artist's books. Fu has created most of her work at fully funded artist residencies such as the Provincetown Fine Arts Work Center, Instituto Sacatar, and the Visual Studies Workshop, and has received many awards for her work, which is included in private and rare archive collections, including the Library of Congress. A passionate educator, she teaches pop-up courses and community workshops with marginalized populations at art centers, universities, and institutions internationally.

TITLE: *Yi Costume Festival*, 2011
DESCRIPTION: Archival ink-jet pop-up book, 17" × 25" × 7" (43.2 × 63.5 × 17.8 cm).

TITLE: *Yao Bride*, 2012
DESCRIPTION: Archival ink-jet pop-up book, 17" × 25" × 5" (43.2 × 63.5 × 12.7 cm).

TITLE: *Ashima*, 2012
DESCRIPTION: Archival ink-jet pop-up book with embroidered Tyvek, 17" × 25" × 13" (43.2 × 63.5 × 33 cm).
Photos: Colette Fu

Hand Papermaking, Inc.

Nonprofit publisher Hand Papermaking has explored and chronicled the art of making paper by hand, showcasing traditional and modern practices worldwide, curating and presenting the best of the field, inspiring the ongoing revival of the craft, and facilitating the emergence of handmade paper as a vibrant contemporary art medium. In addition to its award-winning journal and newsletter, Hand Papermaking is known for its distinctive series of portfolios. Number 9 in the series "Handmade Paper in Motion" features pop-ups, movable devices, and other forms of dynamic paper engineering. The motion and imagery is enhanced physically and conceptually by the use of handmade paper designed and made specifically for each edition.

TITLE: *Pulp Alchemy*, 2010
DESCRIPTION: Handmade paper (from cotton, gingko, papyrus, milkweed, fescue, dracaena fiber), hand cut into petal forms, mounted onto color-laser-printed 80 lb. Coronado SST cover weight paper; original plant illustrations; Gudy O adhesive, 10" × 8" (25.4 × 20.3 cm).

Collaborators: Winnie Radolan and Pamela Wood

TITLE: *Untitled*, 2010
DESCRIPTION: Handmade paper (combination of cotton rag, abaca, cooked flax type R, pigment, mica), pulp painted through stencils with pigmented cotton rag pulp; walnut-dyed base sheets; hand cutting; adhesive; 10" × 16" × 3" (25.4 × 40.6 × 7.6 cm).

Collaborators: Philip Bell and Amy Jacobs

TITLE: *Beware of Gods Bearing Gifts*, 2010
DESCRIPTION: Pigmented flax and Belgium-flax handmade paper, pulp painted, die cut, letterpress printed, folded; riser form; adhesive; string; 19" × 10" × 8" (48.3 × 25.4 × 20.3 cm).

Collaborators: Emily Martin and Bridget O'Malley

Ed Hutchins

Since 1989, Ed Hutchins has been proprietor of Editions, a workshop for producing artist's book multiples. He has taught, lectured, curated shows, directed book arts programs, and created editioned books while traveling across the United States, Canada, Mexico, Australia, and New Zealand. In 2009, he designed and supervised the construction of a small house in the center of a sixty-three-acre nature park that he shares with his spouse, Steve Warren, and Ella the wonder dog.

TITLE: *Maryline's Garden*, 1996
DESCRIPTION: Illustrations pop down between mirrored pages to create kaleidoscope gardens.

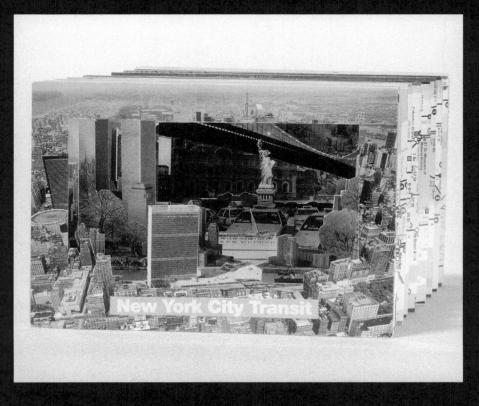

TITLE: *New York City Transit*, 1997
DESCRIPTION: Pre-9/11 postcard tunnel book with travel map hinges.

Photos: Cora DuBack

Sam Ita

Sam Ita is the creator of more than a dozen pop-up book titles. He is best known for a series adapting classical literature to pop-up comics. Inspired by origami, he has also applied his unique abilities to a variety of fields, including animation and toy design. His book, *The Odyssey, a Pop-Up Book*, earned starred reviews from *Publisher's Weekly* and *Kirkus Reviews*.

TITLE: *Statue of Liberty*, 2011
DESCRIPTION: Pop-up card, 3" × 5" (7.6 × 12.7 cm).

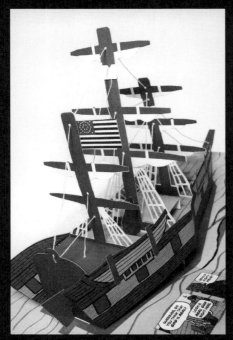

TITLE: *Moby Dick, A Pop-Up Book*, 2007
DESCRIPTION: Sterling Press, publisher, 9¼" × 11½" (23.5 × 29.2 cm).

TITLE: *20,000 Leagues Under the Sea, A Pop-Up Book*, 2008
DESCRIPTION: Sterling Press, publisher, 9¼" × 11½" (23.5 × 29.2 cm).

Photos: Sam Ita

Renee Jablow

Renee Jablow creates pop-up and novelty paper designs for books, cards, advertising, and packaging. After graduating from Claremont McKenna College, she polished her paper engineering skills at Intervisual Books (Piggy Toes Press) where she worked for thirteen years. While there, she paper engineered more than sixty books for clients such as Disney Press, Universal Studios, DreamWorks, Simon & Schuster, and Scholastic. Renee currently does freelance paper engineering from her home office in Los Angeles. A highlight of her paper engineering career was nominated for a Grammy Award for Best Recording Package for The Ditty Bops's *Summer Rains* pop-up CD package.

TITLE: *Water Lily*, 2012
DESCRIPTION: Published by Up With Paper, LLC, paper-engineered by Renee Jablow, illustrated by Katie Scheid, 5¼" × 5¼" (13.3 × 13.3 cm).

TITLE: *Valentine Owls*, 2011
DESCRIPTION: Published by Up With Paper, LLC, paper-engineered by Renee Jablow, illustrated by Colleen O'Hara, 5¼" × 5¼" (13.3 × 13.3 cm).

TITLE: *Wedding Carriage*, 2012
DESCRIPTION: Published by Up With Paper, LLC, paper-engineered by Renee Jablow, illustrated by Chris Lyons, 9¼" × 3¾" (23.5 × 9.5 cm).

Photos: Aaron Borchetta

Paul Johnson

England–based Paul Johnson is recognized internationally for his pioneering work in developing literacy through the book arts and as a book artist. He is the author of more than fifteen titles, and his unique pop-up books are represented in most of the major collections in the United States. Johnson specializes in unique sculptural pop-up books that have no folds—instead, paper dovetails and interlocking joints connect all of the sections. His inspiration comes from medieval European religious art, the art of Southeast Asia, and the buildings of the Spanish architect Gaudí.

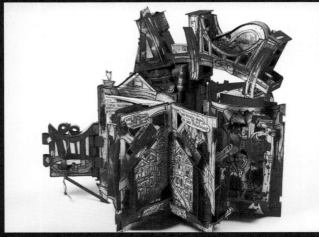

TITLE: *Old Mother Hubbard in San Francisco*, 2013
DESCRIPTION: Unique 360-degree carousel pop-up book, 15" × 13" × 4" (38 × 33 × 10.2 cm) (closed).

TITLE: *Old Mother Hubbard in San Francisco*, 2013
DESCRIPTION: Unique 360-degree carousel pop-up book, 15" × 13" × 4" (38 × 33 × 10.2 cm) (closed).

TITLE: *Noah's Ark*, 2013
DESCRIPTION: Unique 180-degree pop-up book, 17" × 26" × 24" (43.2 × 66 × 61 cm).

Photos: Mike Black

Yoojin Kim

Yoojin Kim is a paper engineer, book artist, printmaker, and designer. She integrates magical properties of pop-ups into most of her creative work. Kim is always looking for inspiration and often investigates the way things fold and how everyday mechanics can apply to pop-ups. She works mostly with imagery of botanical biomorphic forms, translating them to interactive paper sculptures. Kim grew up in Japan and Korea where she learned to appreciate paper folding by making origami trinkets.

TITLE: *(flightless) Avian Osteology*, 2013
DESCRIPTION: Paper-cut pop-up book, 11" × 14" × 9" (28 × 35.6 × 23 cm).

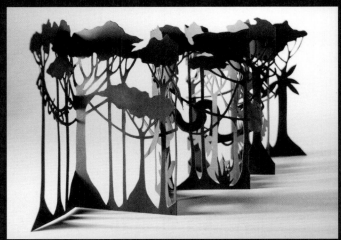

TITLE: *Entwined*, 2010
DESCRIPTION: Paper-cut accordion book, 3" × 7" × 12" (7.6 × 17.8 × 30.5 cm).

TITLE: *Entwined*
DESCRIPTION: Paper-cut accordion book, 3" × 7" × 12" (7.6 × 17.8 × 30.5 cm).
Photos: Yoojin Kim

Emily Martin

Emily Martin has been making movable and sculptural artist's books since the late 1970s. Her books are narrative (sometimes autobiographical) and make use of format as a metaphor for content. Martin lives in Iowa City, Iowa, where she has her studio and also teaches at the University of Iowa Center for the Book. Her work is in public and private collections throughout the United States and internationally, including the Metropolitan Museum of Art, New York; the Victoria and Albert Museum, London; The Museum of Contemporary Art Chicago; The Marvin and Ruth Sackner Archive of Concrete and Visual Poetry, Miami; and others.

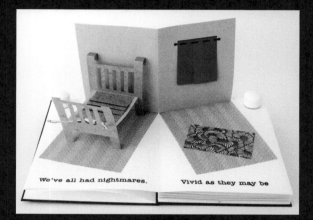

TITLE: *Sleepers, Dreamers & Screamers*, 2006
DESCRIPTION: An accordion pop-up book, printed letterpress with hard covers enclosed in a matching clamshell box. The pop-ups are constructed of a variety of papers including a cotton and gampi paper made for the project by Bridget O'Malley of Cave Paper. Edition of fifteen. 9½" × 7" (24 × 17.8 cm).

Photos: Barry Phipps

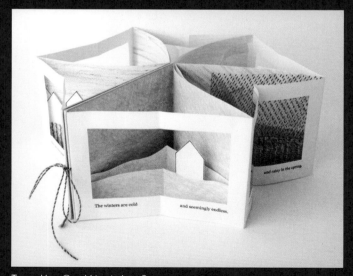

TITLE: *How Can I Live in Iowa?*, 1999
DESCRIPTION: A carousel book with six scenes and text, archival ink-jet printed on Mohawk Superfine and transparency film, case bound with Nideggen paper, laser printed title, cord tie closure. Number four of the five books of the Iowa series. Edition of twenty-five. 5" × 6¾" (12.7 × 17 cm).

TITLE: *Sleepers, Dreamers & Screamers*, 2006
DESCRIPTION: The complete text is "We've all had nightmares. Vivid as they may be there is always that sweet release upon waking. But what happens when events in our waking lives surpass even our most horrific dreams. Where is our release now?" This book was begun in 2001 and derailed by the events of September 11, 2001. The text was rewritten in the aftermath and finally completed. 9½" × 7" (24 × 17.8 cm).

Kyle Olmon

Kyle Olmon is an American children's pop-up book creator and author. His first major project was *Celebration*, a collaborative pop-up book sponsored by The Movable Book Society. Afterward, Olmon worked with Robert Sabuda and Matthew Reinhart for eight years. He is the author and designer of *The New York Times* best-selling pop-up book, *Castle: Medieval Days* and *Knights* and *Baby Signs: A Pop-Up Book*. Olmon regularly partners with individuals and organizations on pop-up projects and exhibitions, both artistic and commercial. He teaches a course on pop-up design at Pratt Institute and is a board member of The Movable Book Society.

TITLE: *Baby Signs*, 2009
DESCRIPTION: Commercial pop-up book, card stock, 7½" × 7½" × 1¾" (19 × 19 × 4.4 cm).

TITLE: *Castle*, 2006
DESCRIPTION: Commercial pop-up book, cardstock, 7¾" × 9¼" × 2¼" (19.7 × 23.5 × 5.7 cm).

TITLE: *Hypnoses*, 2013
DESCRIPTION: Pop-up press kit, card stock, 12" × 10" × 1¼" (30.5 × 25.4 × 3.2 cm).

Photos: Kyle Olmon

David Pelham

London–based David Pelham began his career in book and magazine production in the early 1960s in England and a decade later wrote and designed his award-winning best seller *The Penguin Book of Kites*, which remains in print to this day. In 1982, in collaboration with polymath Dr. Jonathan Miller, he designed and produced the hugely successful award-winning *The Human Body*, which brought pop-up techniques to a new and far wider market. Pelham worked as creative director of Intervisual Books, generating ideas for countless novelty titles and overseeing its production in Los Angeles, Colombia, and Mexico.

TITLE: *Trail*, 2007
DESCRIPTION: Published by Simon & Schuster; author, designer, illustrator, and paper engineer: David Pelham; 8¼" × 8¼" (21 x 21 cm); a complex all-white pop-up book featuring a winding trail that the reader follows throughout the book.

TITLE: *Say Cheese*, 1998
DESCRIPTION: Published by Jonathan Cape Limited, UK; author, designer, illustrator, and paper engineer: David Pelham; 5" × 5½" (12.7 × 14 cm). A wedge-shaped book resembling a slice of cheese with a three-dimensional mouse built into the cover. A pop-up story of mice who are not enjoying a party until the photographer says, "Say cheese!" after which the party proceeds with a swing.

Jie Qi

Jie Qi received a bachelor of science in mechanical engineering at Columbia University and worked in electronics design and fabrication at Eyebeam Art + Technology Center on the littleBits project. Qi is currently a doctoral student in the Responsive Environments Group at the Massachusetts Institute of Technology Media Lab. Her research investigates materials and techniques for blending electronics with traditional arts and crafts media to create personally meaningful technology. Her interest lies in the questions that arise when we use circuits and programming, that is, interactivity and logic, to express ourselves. What magical experiences can these techniques and materials enable? What new stories can we tell?

TITLE: *Electronic Popables*, 2009
DESCRIPTION: Paper-based electronics, magnetic circuit boards, 8" × 10" × 6" (20.3 × 25.4 × 15.2 cm) (open). Purple page: A bend sensor in the sailboat detects when it is lifted, causing the city's skyline to light up.

Photos: Leah Buechley

TITLE: *Electronic Popables*, 2009
DESCRIPTION: Paper-based electronics, magnetic circuit boards, 8" × 10" × 6" (20.3 × 25.4 × 15.2 cm) (open). Pink page: Pull tabs act as mechanical and electrical switches causing flowers to move and glow and the bumblebee to twinkle as it flies up and down.

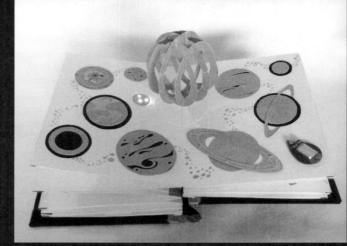

TITLE: *Electronic Popables*, 2009
DESCRIPTION: Paper-based electronics, magnetic circuit boards, 8" × 10" × 6" (20.3 × 25.4 × 15.2 cm) (open). Yellow page: Pressing on the various planets triggers lights to glow on the pop-up sun and planets. When you press on Mars, Venus vibrates using a pager motor. When you press on Pluto, the sun shines brighter.

Shawn Sheehy

Shawn Sheehy combines paper engineering with an interest in biological and cultural evolution to produce sculptural pop-up books. Sheehy has taught workshops at the Paper & Book Intensive, Penland, the Centers for Book Arts in Chicago and New York, and many other venues across the United States. His commercial pop-up clients include the American Girl Company, American Greetings, and *The Pee-Wee Herman Show on Broadway*. He's currently at work on a project to be published by Candlewick in 2015.

TITLE: *Hummingbird* (from *Welcome to the NeighborWood: A Pop-Up Book of Animal Architecture*), 2004
DESCRIPTION: Letterpress, handmade paper, construction, 14" × 10" × 8¾" (35.6 × 25.4 × 22.2 cm) (open).

Photo: Julia Stotz

TITLE: *Mice* (from *Beyond the 6th Extinction: A Fifth Millennium Bestiary*), 2007
DESCRIPTION: Letterpress, handmade paper, construction, 14" × 9" × 10¼" (35.6 × 23 × 26 cm) (open).

TITLE: *Pigeon* (from *Beyond the 6th Extinction: A Fifth Millennium Bestiary*), 2007
DESCRIPTION: Letterpress, handmade paper, construction, 14" × 9" × 10¼" (35.6 × 23 × 26 cm) (open).

Photos: Ricardo Martinez

Robert Sabuda

Robert Sabuda saw his first pop-up book in the waiting room of his dentist's office when he was a kid growing up in Michigan. He began illustrating children's books while in college at Pratt Institute in New York City.

In the early 1990s, he started thinking about working in three dimensions and remembered his love of pop-ups. He began taking pop-up books apart in order to understand the challenges of their geometry and construction. He came up with the idea for his first pop-up book, *The Christmas Alphabet*. The first publisher he showed the book to loved the concept, but declined the book because they didn't know how to produce it. Sabuda wasn't deterred. He took it to another publisher that didn't know how to produce it either, but thought the book was such a great idea that it took on the project.

Sabuda and his editor were taking a big gamble on this book. Most books at the time were illustrated in full color, but Sabuda wanted to create a pop-up book in stark white paper, allowing the shapes, shadows, and the "wow" factor of the pop-ups to be the central attraction. And at a retail cost of $19.99 (£13), this was an expensive children's book; even the publisher's sales reps didn't think they could sell it. Fortunately for Sabuda and his editor, the book turned out to be a big hit, proving that you can't underestimate what the general public will purchase.

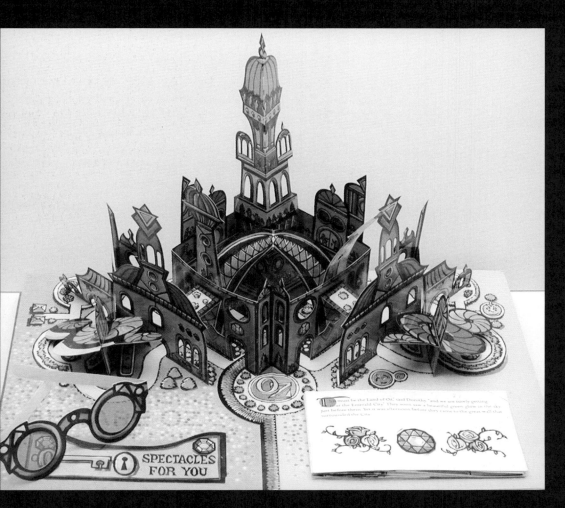

TITLE: *The Wonderful Wizard of Oz*, 2000
DESCRIPTION: This glorious edition is told in a shorter version of L. Frank Baum's original text, with artwork in the style of W. W. Denslow. With sparkling touches of colored foil and Emerald City eyeglasses, this classic tale is certain to find an honored place on the family bookshelf, published by Simon & Schuster.

Photos: Robert Sabuda

The success of this book launched Sabuda's career. He tends to create all aspects of his books and calls himself a bookmaker: He writes the text, draws the illustrations, and does the paper engineering. He has published more than thirty pop-up books, some of them starting out with an initial print run of half a million copies.

Sabuda works in his New York studio where he creates one or two new pop-up books a year, produces a line of cards and stationery for the Museum of Modern Art, and is spearheading the renovation of an old barn upstate, which he is turning into an artist space with studios and a gallery. He isn't afraid the digital world will eliminate pop-up books, saying that he meets a lot of parents (including me!) who would prefer to put a pop-up book, rather than an electronic device, into the hands of their children.

Title: *The 12 Days of Christmas,* 1996
Description: A true holiday classic literally comes to life in this stunning pop-up edition of a seasonal favorite, published by Simon & Schuster.

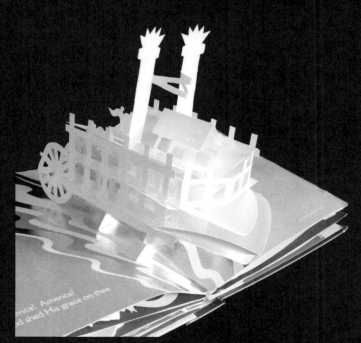

Title: *America the Beautiful,* 2004
Description: From the Golden Gate Bridge to Mount Rushmore to the Statue of Liberty, America has never looked more spectacular, published by Simon & Schuster.

Title: *Alice's Adventures in Wonderland,* 2003
Description: This is one of Sabuda's most amazing creations ever, featuring stunning pop-ups, published by Simon & Schuster.

Dorothy A. Yule

Dorothy A. Yule has taught book arts at the Academy of Art University in San Francisco and pop-up and movable book structures at the California College of the Arts in Oakland. She often collaborates with her twin sister, Susan Hunt Yule, on books produced under her imprint, Left Coast Press, two of which were published as trade books by Chronicle Books (*Souvenir of New York* and *Souvenir of San Francisco*). Her books are in museums and special collections, including those of the Cooper-Hewitt Museum in New York; the Museum of the Book in The Hague; the Victoria and Albert Museum in London; and the Walker Art Center in Minneapolis.

TITLE: *Memories of Science*, 2012
DESCRIPTION: Close-up of Science Magnet.
Photos: Ed Rachles

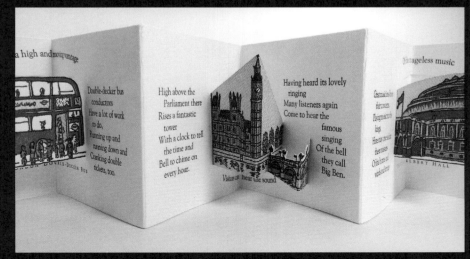

TITLE: *Souvenirs of Great Cities: New York, San Francisco, Paris, and London* (detail of London).

TO LEARN MORE ABOUT POP-UPS

There are both private and public collections of pop-ups and movable books around the world. The private ones are often off-limits to the public. Occasionally these collections can be seen on exhibition, and collectors sometimes write about their expertise. Collector Ann Montanaro even founded an organization dedicated to pop-ups and movables. She founded The Movable Book Society in 1992, an organization dedicated to pop-ups and movables. Her collection is quite large, focusing on English-language publications, which she documents through a newsletter. Her favorite pop-up book is Robert Sabuda's *Cookie Count* (see below).

There are a growing number of special collections in libraries (often in special collections departments or rare book rooms) that collect pop-ups, as well as artists' books and other rare materials. These libraries are generally open to the public by appointment, and you can often view exhibitions featuring the works they own, sometimes accompanied by works on loan. These libraries are a wonderful resource for those interested in seeing old pop-ups that are no longer in print or available for purchase. Increasingly, these collections are being cataloged online as well.

When Montanaro began her research on pop-ups and movable books in the 1980s, she discovered not much had been written about them. She began assembling a bibliography of pop-ups and movables (the first two volumes are available from Scarecrow Press), and later she authored a history of pop-ups, which appears in the book *Making Pop-Ups and Novelty Cards*.

She also publishes a quarterly newsletter, called *Movable Stationery*. The group engages paper engineers and book artists as well as collectors and holds meetings in various places around the United States, allowing members to visit collections and interact with movable book professionals and enthusiasts from around the country.

For more information, see the Resources on page 143.

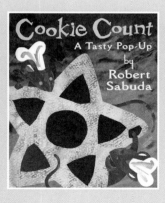

Templates

Templates copyright individual artists . Photocopy at 100% unless otherwise noted.
Access downloadable project templates at www.quarrybooks.com/pages/pop-ups.

Pop-Up Paper Earrings, *page 39*

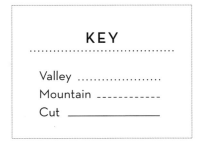

KEY

Valley ....
Mountain - - - - - - - - -
Cut _____

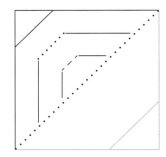

Tower of Babel, *page 41*

KEY

Valley _____
Mountain _____
Cut _____

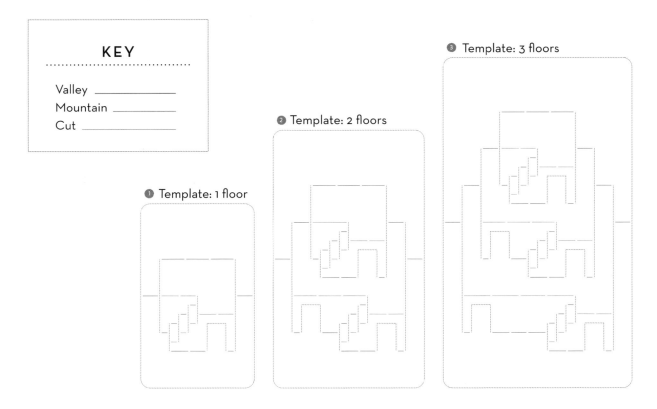

❸ Template: 3 floors

❷ Template: 2 floors

❶ Template: 1 floor

Photocopy at 200%.

Pop-Up City Skyline, *page 47*

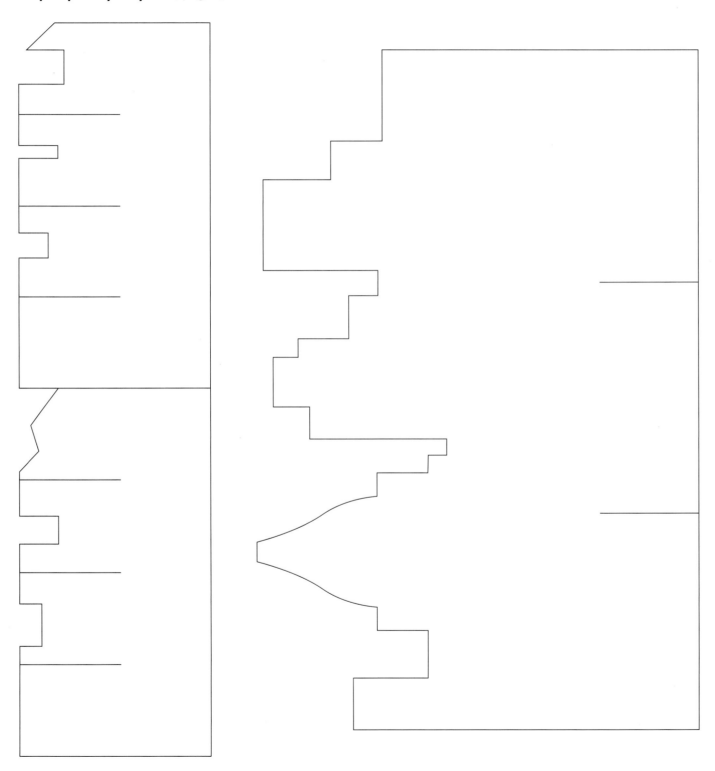

Pop-Up City Skyline *(continued), page 47*

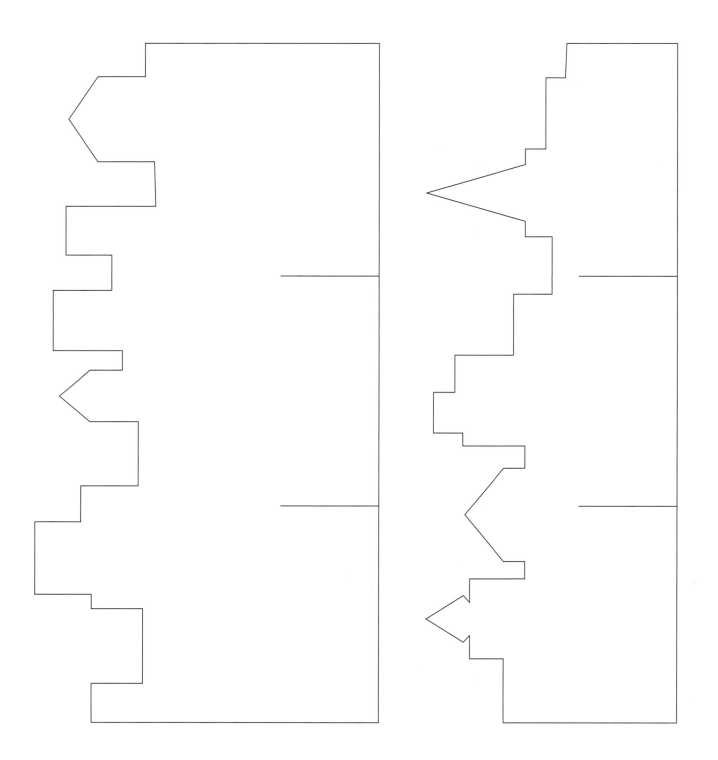

Pop-Up Valentine, *page 51*

KEY

Valley ....
Mountain -- -- -- -- --
Cut _____

Photocopy at 200%.

Pop-Up Robot, *page 53*

KEY

Valley -- -- -- -- --
Mountain -- · -- · -- ·
Cut _____

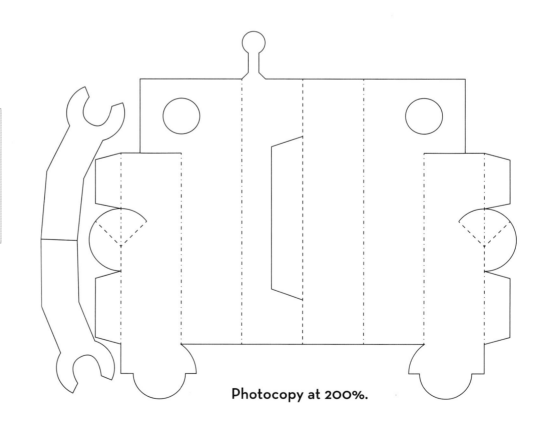

Photocopy at 200%.

Bloodroot Plant, *page 55*

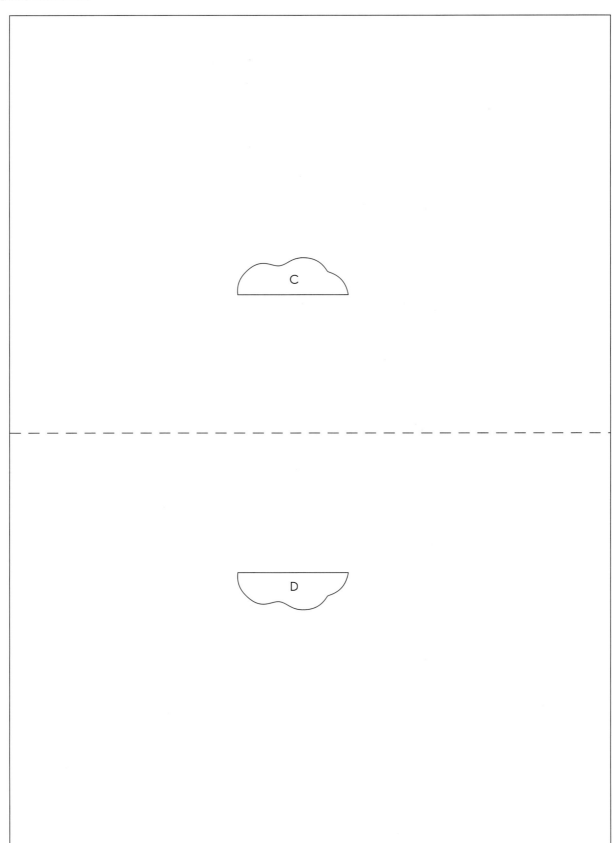

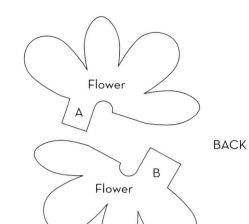

KEY

Valley _ _ _ _ _

Mountain - - - - - - - -

Cut _____

Flower

A

Flower

B

BACK

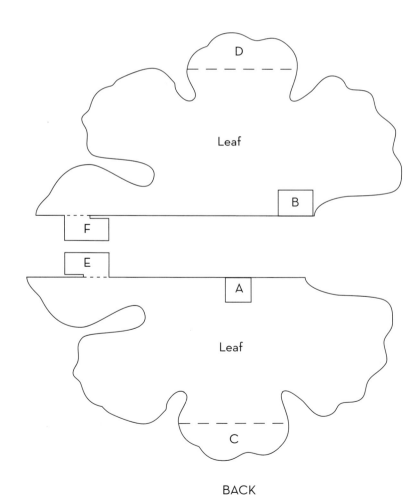

D

Leaf

B

F

E

A

Leaf

C

BACK

Pop-Up Dragon, *page 57*

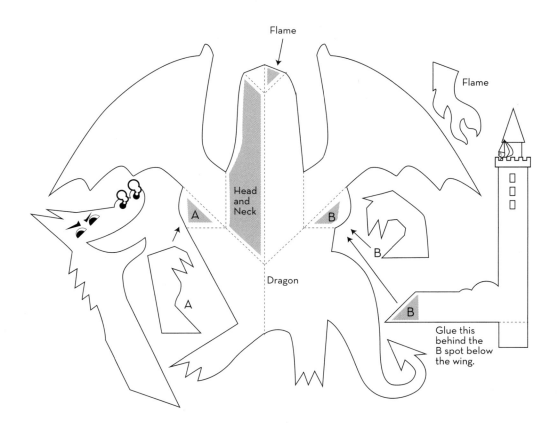

Photocopy at 200%.

Base card front

KEY

···················

Score and fold --------
Cut _____

Base card back

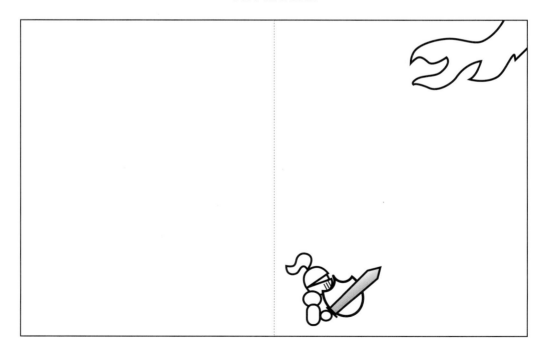

Photocopy all at 200%.

Pop-Up First Bank, *page 60*

Top Layer

Photocopy at 200%.

Middle Layer

Photocopy at 200%.

Bottom Layer

Photocopy at 200%.

Pop-Up Tent and Pyramid, *page 65*

3-Dimensional Equilateral Tent

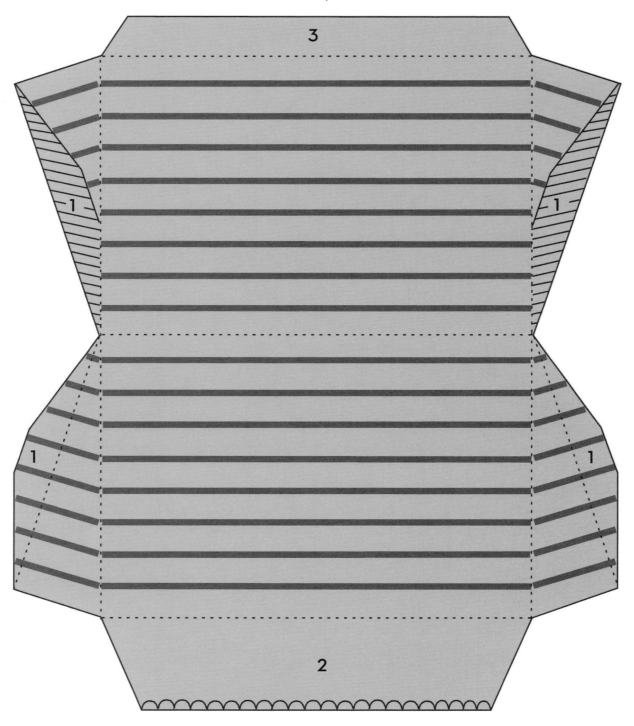

3-Dimensional Equilateral Pyramid

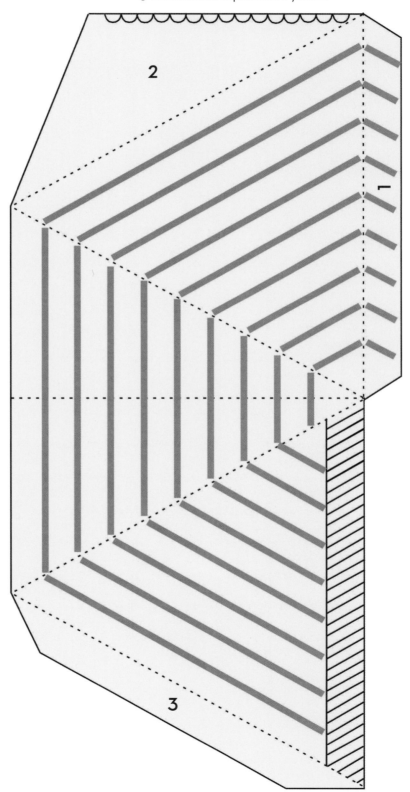

KEY
....

Fold ---------
Glue //////

2

1

3

Carousel Pop-Up Book, *page 68*

Floor

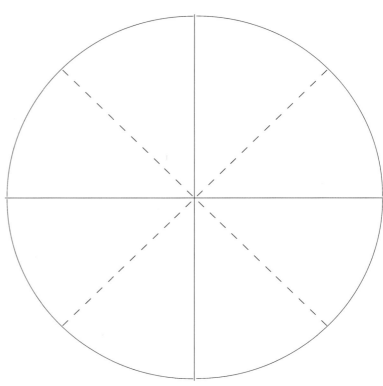

Kitchen Walls

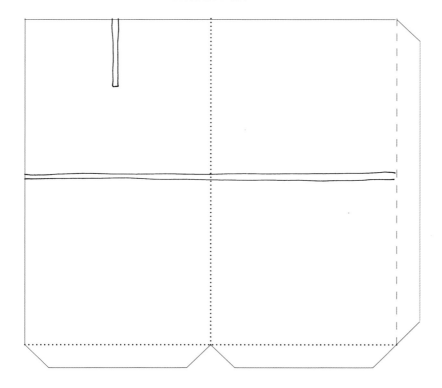

Photocopy all at 200%.

Bedroom Walls

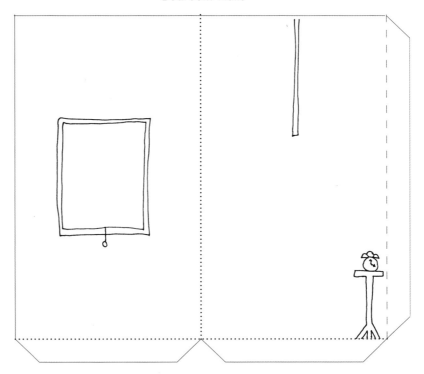

KEY

Valley . . . .

Mountain _ _ _ _

Outdoor Grill Walls

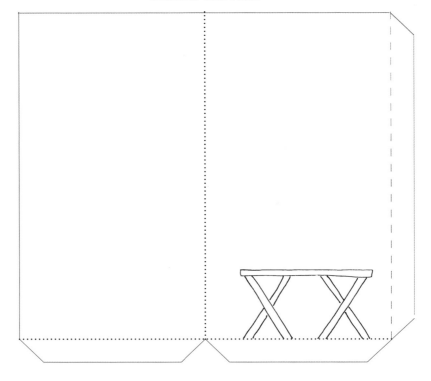

Photocopy all at 200%.

Carousel Pop-Up Book (continued), *page 68*

Outdoor Laundry Walls

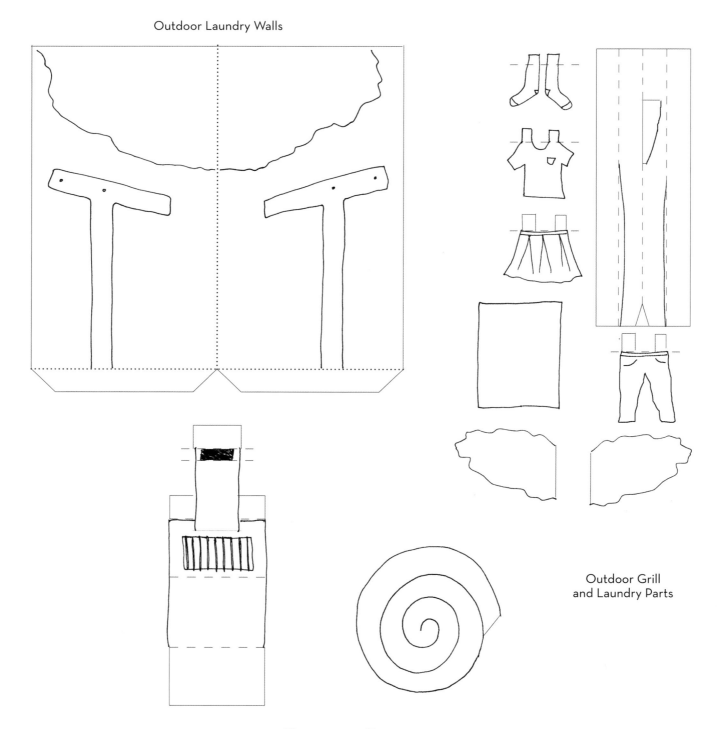

Outdoor Grill
and Laundry Parts

Photocopy all at 200%.

Bedroom Parts

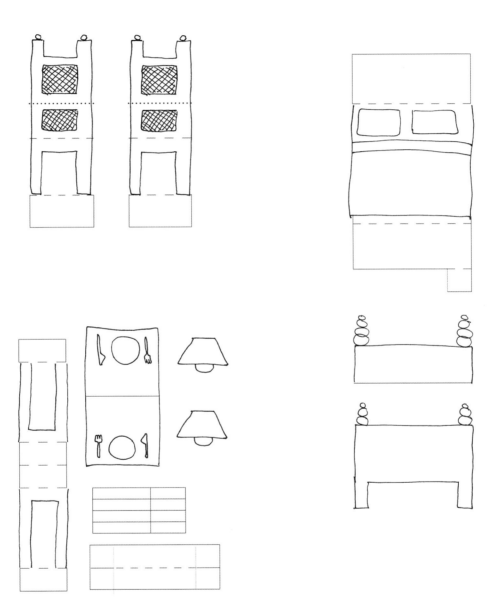

Photocopy all at 200%.

Puppy Puppet, *page 81*

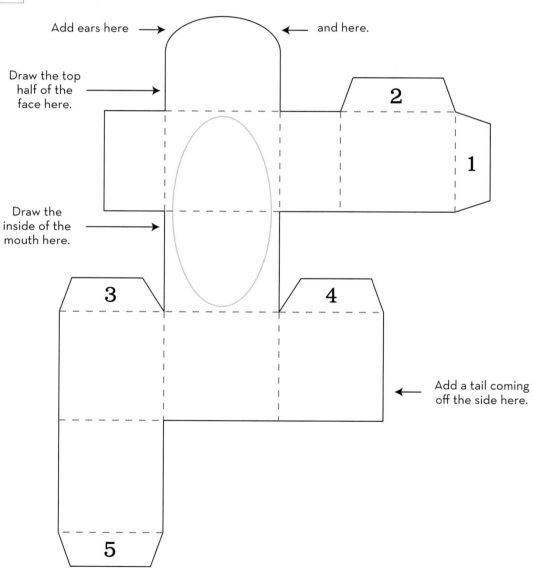

KEY

Cut ——————

Fold — — — — — —

FRONT

Add ears here → ← and here.

Draw the top half of the face here. →

2

1

Draw the inside of the mouth here. →

3

4

Add a tail coming off the side here. ←

5

BACK

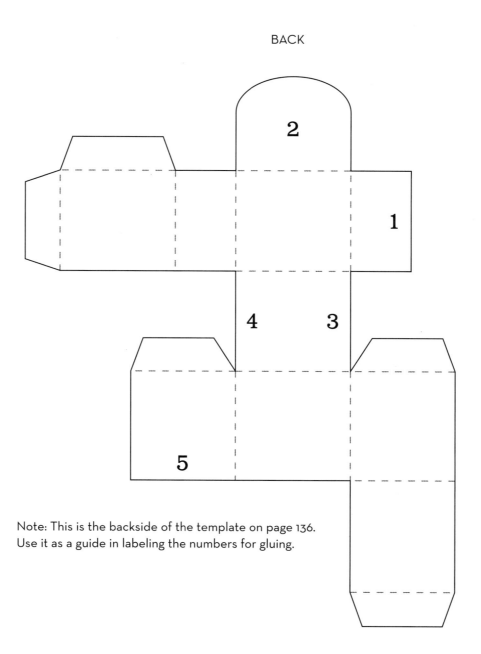

Note: This is the backside of the template on page 136.
Use it as a guide in labeling the numbers for gluing.

Pull-Tab Rib Cage, *page 81*

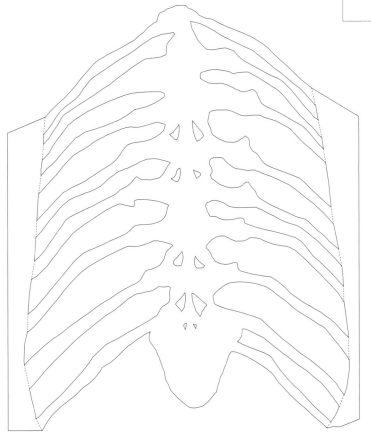

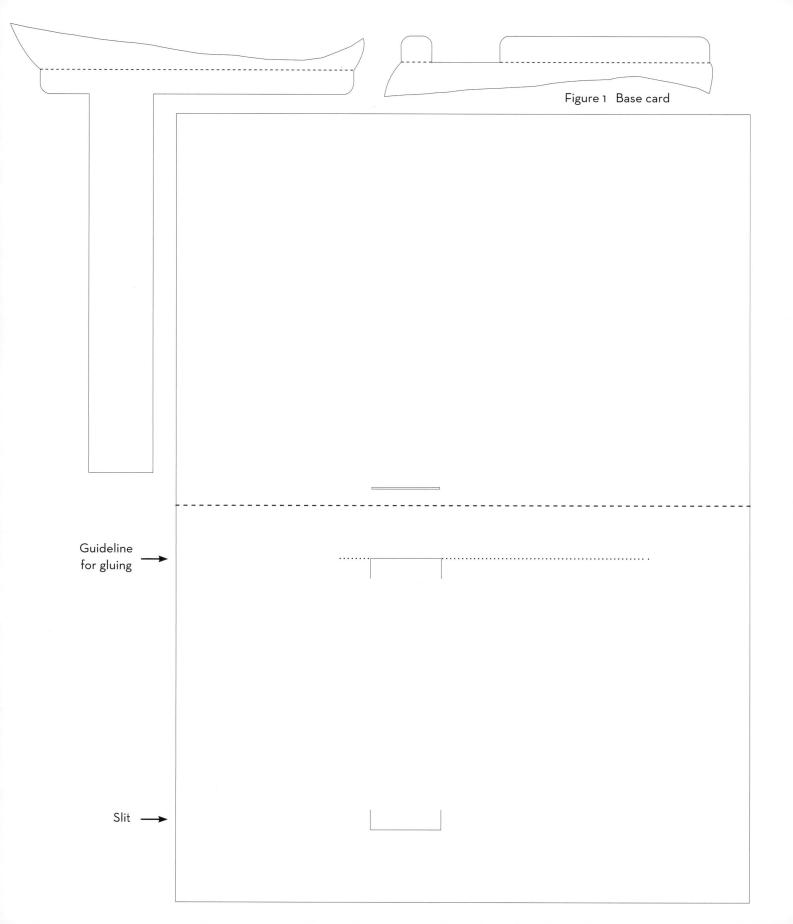

Figure 1 Base card

Guideline
for gluing →

Slit →

Tunnel Book, *page 76*

Volvelle with Six Slots, *page 85*

Note: All lines appear on the back side of the wheel.

Volvelle with six slots, part 1

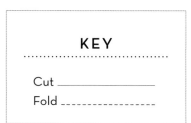

```
KEY
..........................................
Cut _____
Fold _ _ _ _ _ _ _ _ _ _
```

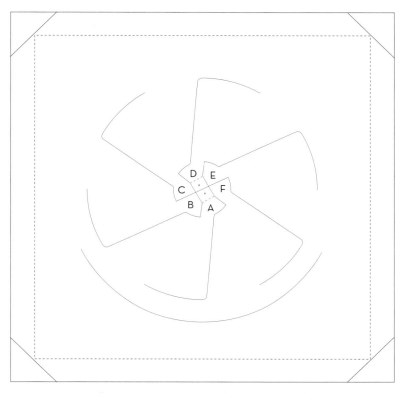

Outer square is 8" x 8" (20.3 x 20.3 cm).

Volvelle with six slots, Part 2

Photocopy all at 200%.

Artist Directory

Shelby Arnold
Brooklyn, NY
www.shelbymakes.com

Tom Bannister
Hand Papermaking, Inc.
Beltsville, MD
www.handpapermaking.org

Andrew Baron
Popyrus Studio, Inc.
Santa Fe, NM
www.popyrus.com

Carol Barton
Glen Echo, MD
www.popularkinetics.com

Marion Bataille
Paris, France
www.marionbataille.com

Elod Beregszaszi
London, England
www.popupology.co.uk

Monika Brandrup
Up With Paper
Mason, OH
www.upwithpaper.com

David Carter
Auburn, CA
www.cartermultimedia.us.com

Julie Chen
Flying Fish Press
Berkeley, CA
www.flyingfishpress.com

Mary Beth Cryan
Woonsocket, RI
www.marybethcryan.com

Peter Dahmen
Dortmund, Germany
www.peterdahmen.de

Bruce Foster
Paperpops
Houston, TX
www.paperpops.com

Colette Fu
Philadelphia, PA
www.colettefu.com

Helen Hiebert
Edwards, CO
www.helenhiebertstudio.com

Ed Hutchins
Salem, NY
www.artistbooks.com

Sam Ita
Brooklyn, NY
www.samita.us

Renee Jablow
Los Angeles, CA
www.reneejablow.com

Paul Johnson
Cheshire, England
www.bookart.co.uk

Yoojin Kim
New Haven, CT
www.yoojinkim.com

Kyle Olmon
Brooklyn, NY
www.kyleolmon.com

David Pelham
London, England

Jie Qi
Cambridge, MA
www.technolojie.com

Robert Sabuda
New York, NY
www.robertsabuda.com

Shawn Sheehy
Chicago, IL
www.shawnsheehy.com

Dorothy A. Yule
Left Coast Press
Oakland, CA
www.leftcoastpress.com

Resources

Specialty supplies featured throughout the book can be found at the following stores and suppliers:

Stores and Supplies

Discount Card Stock
Salt Lake City, UT
www.discountcardstock.com
Colored card stocks at discounted prices (card and letter sizes)

The Lamp Shop
www.lampshop.com
Glue applicators

Talas
www.talasonline.com
Papers and bookbinding supplies

Books

The Art of Pop-Up: The Magical World of Three-Dimensional Books
Jean-Charles Trebbi
Promopress

This book features the designs and innovations of paper engineers from around the world.

The Elements of Pop-Up: A Pop-Up Book for Aspiring Paper Engineers
David A. Carter and James Diaz
Little Simon

This book features basic and complex mechanisms through pop-up illustrations, so that you can study the construction of various pop-up mechanisms as you unfold the pages in the book.

New Pop-Up Paper Projects
Paul Johnson
Routledge

This book guides you through basic techniques and foundation skills, offers advice on classroom planning, health, and safety, and shows you how to ensure that learners of all ages can develop and progress their skills.

The Paper Architect
Marivi Garrido and Ingrid Siliakus
Potter Craft US, realized by Ivy Press UK

This book features architectural origami, where a single sheet of paper is cut and folded into an intricate miniature structure. Here, three of the world's leading proponents provide instructions and templates for re-creating twenty of the world's great buildings, from the Taj Mahal to the Rialto Bridge. There are basic principles to start you off, as well as galleries of the finest architectural origami from around the world.

The Pocket Paper Engineer,
Volumes 1, 2, and 3
Carol Barton
Popular Kinetics Press

The *Pocket Paper Engineer*, Volume 1, is a lively how-to workbook that guides the reader through the process of designing and constructing basic pop-up forms. Volume 2 covers four important glued pop-up structures: platforms, props, spirals, and straddles. Volume 3 covers the most amazing V-fold pop-up and its many variations.

The Pop-Up Book: Step-by-Step Instructions for Creating Over 100 Original Paper Projects
Paul Jackson
Henry Holt & Company, Inc.

The Pop-Up Book is a clear and practical guide to the craft of the three-dimensional paper movement, illustrated with full-color photography.

Pop-Up Design and Paper Mechanics: How to Make Folding Paper Sculpture
Duncan Birmingham
Guild of Master Craftsman Publications Ltd.

This book provides comprehensive information on the geometry of pop-ups, so that you understand how they work.

Pop-Up: Everything You Need to Know to Create Your Own Pop-Up Book
Ruth Wickings and Frances Castle
Quarto Children's Books

In this book, you punch out pages and assemble pop-ups, creating a new book and learning pop-up techniques during the process.

The Practical Step-by-Step Guide to Making Pop-Up & Novelty Cards: A Masterclass in the Art of Paper Engineering
Trish Phillips and Ann Montanaro
Arness Publishing, Ltd. (2011)
This book begins with an excellent history of pop-ups and movables and is filled with how-to projects.

These books are out of print but are worth looking for through used book dealers:

Pop-Up Geometric Origami
Masahiro Chatani
Ondorisha Publishers, Ltd.

Pop-Up Origamic Architecture
Masahiro Chatani
Ondorisha Publishers, Ltd.

Websites

I encourage you to explore the websites of the artists listed in the Artist Directory (page 142). Many of them have templates that you can download and print out on their sites.

Movable Book Society
www.movablebooksociety.org

The Movable Book Society is a membership organization that provides a forum for collectors, artists, curators, booksellers, book producers, and others to share enthusiasm and exchange information about pop-up and movable books. The society holds a biennial conference and publishes a quarterly newsletter.

About the Author

Helen Hiebert runs a small papermaking studio near Vail, Colorado, where she creates art, installations, and artist's books, trains interns, and hosts workshops and consultations. She teaches and lectures internationally, sharing her passion for paper. She is the author of *Playing with Paper, Papermaking with Garden Plants & Common Weeds, The Papermaker's Companion*, and *Paper Illuminated* and the producer of the films *Water Paper Time* and *The Papermaker's Studio Guide*.

Acknowledgments

I am grateful to all of the paper engineers and artists who were willing to share their knowledge with us: to those who contributed their unique projects and provided images of their majestic paper creations. Special thanks to my editor, Mary Ann Hall, for recommending me for this project, and to Zach Mahone for his artistry in capturing the projects in photos. And to Ann Montanaro and Shawn Sheehy, thank you for providing me with your guidance, enthusiasm, and support as I navigated my way through this fine field.